AF844054

CONTENTS

Introduction 5
Patterns of Attendance 9
The Status of the Jurors 15
The Evolution of the Grand Jury 20
Swearing and Charging 21
Presentments 24
The Growth of Grand Jury Independence 33
The Grand Jury and the Great Rebellion 39
Cheshire and Elsewhere: Some Comparisons 41
Conclusion 45
Notes 48
Appendix I. A Note on the Sources 54
Appendix II. Statistics 56
Appendix III. A Note on the Head Constables 59
Map: Cheshire: hundreds and sessions towns 8

NOTE ON TRANSCRIPTION

In quotations standard abbreviations have been expanded. Otherwise the original spelling and punctuation have been retained.

ABBREVIATIONS

Brit. Mus., Add. MS.	British Museum, Additional MS.
Brit. Mus., Harl. MS.	British Museum, Harleian MS.
C.R.O., Q.J.F.	Cheshire Record Office, Quarter Sessions File
C.R.O., Quarter Sessions Book	Cheshire Record Office, Quarter Sessions Book (6a, 9a, books of orders and recognizances) (7a, 8a, 10a, books of indictments and presentments)
P.R.O., Chester 21	Public Record Office, Cheshire Assize Order Books
P.R.O., Chester 24	Public Record Office, Cheshire Assize Rolls

These assize records are kept at the Public Record Office's depository at Ashridge.

£3.95

G2W

Department of English Local History

OCCASIONAL PAPERS

Third Series Edited by Alan Everitt

Number 1

The Cheshire Grand Jury 1625–1659

A Social and Administrative Study

by J. S. MORRILL
Fellow and Director of Studies in History,
Selwyn College, Cambridge

372416

LEICESTER UNIVERSITY PRESS 1976

First published in 1976 by Leicester University Press

Copyright © J. S. Morrill 1976

All rights reserved. No part of this publication may be reproduced, stored in a retrieval system, or transmitted, in any form or by any means, electronic, mechanical, photocopying, recording or otherwise, without the prior permission of the Leicester University Press.

Printed and bound in Great Britain by Unwin Brothers Ltd, The Gresham Press, Old Woking, Surrey

ISBN 0 7185 2031 9

INTRODUCTION

> For the great Inquest at the Quarter Sessions, the sherife of the Countie returneth by warrant, two, or three out of every hundred, of the most discreet, hable, and sufficient persons, both for their estates, and understanding, of wch choyce is made by the Justices of the peace, to the number of 17, 19 or 21 to receive the Indictments, or of their own knowledge to present any offenders against his Majesties lawes; and the like course hath hitherto ben used at the Assizes, for that such persons are better acquainted with the comon grievance of the Countrie, then Justices are.

This anonymous undated opinion, long since forgotten amidst the miscellanea of the Jacobean Privy Council,[1] comes closer to offering a succinct and accurate account of the nature of the seventeenth-century grand jury than anything else published at the time or since. Despite the plethora of studies on Stuart local government which have appeared, including some specifically concerned with the work of the court of quarter sessions, the grand jury has never received detailed attention. It has not been completely ignored; some of the generally sound introductions to quarter sessions records calandared for many counties have given brief accounts of the grand jury system, but it is revealing that most of those accounts simply quote one another or rely on the handbooks prepared for local governors by sixteenth-or seventeenth-century lawyers, notably Lambarde's Eirenarcha, Dalton's Office and Authority of Sheriffs, or the anonymous Office of the Clerk of Assize. Neither these introductions nor any of the published and unpublished theses on local government have made any systematic attempt to employ local sources to extend our knowledge of the workings of the grand jury system. What we have, then, are little more than accounts of the juries' conventional and statutory duties and powers, usually with a few random examples of their work. There is need of a systematic analysis of their activities, and above all need of an attempt to estimate the significance of the grand jury system within the general context of local government. Was it already, as it had certainly become long before its final abolition in the second quarter of the twentieth century, a minor and insignificant part in the formal legal process, or was its role more vital and creative? By default, historians appear to have assumed the former. This study is an attempt to elucidate these questions. It is based on the remarkably full grand jury lists and presentment rolls from both assizes and quarter sessions for Cheshire for the years 1617-65,[2] although detailed analysis is restricted to the period 1625-59.[3]

The pattern is reasonably clear. Grand juries were drawn from the lowest ranks of the gentry and many jurors were required to serve time after time. Their functions included the finding of indictments and the remarkably open-ended making of presentments. Indictments had a purely technical, legal function; the jurors were provided with summaries of the charges and evidence against suspected persons and they determined whether there was a case to be answered. Only when a grand jury had endorsed the bill of accusation could the court proceed to trial before justices and jury. The other formal duty of the grand jury was the making of presentments, that is, the notification of the court of administrative or criminal defaults known to them. The jury also possessed less well-defined and less regular powers to proceed as 'the body of the county'; whenever the community wished to complain to a higher authority, such as the Privy Council or Parliament, the grand jury would be asked to initiate or to endorse a petition. There is no doubt that a convention existed by which the grand jury were accepted as the authoritative voice of county opinion. A grand jury petition carried more weight even than a petition of the justices of the peace. Much of this paper is concerned to suggest that the proper performance of these duties was of fundamental importance to the operation of county government.

The extent to which every county developed a distinctive pattern of local government is all too frequently overlooked. It is clear that both in its procedures and in its enforcement of economic and social policy, each county gave as much weight to local precedents and customs as it did to the terms of a statute or the expectations of the Privy Council. This is as true of the role of juries as it is of the operation of the poor law or local responses to Charles I's Book of Orders. At the end of this study there will be an attempt to establish some of the principal differences between Cheshire and other counties with regard to the grand jury system. But it is as well to establish at the outset that neither Cheshire nor any other county can be taken as typical.

It will be necessary to begin, however, by outlining those elements in the general administrative structure of Cheshire which make it distinctive. First and foremost among these must be the status of Cheshire as a county palatine. Despite Henry VIII's assaults on the independence of ancient jurisdictions, Cheshire retained its own system of courts which largely set it apart from the national framework. Thus the Exchequer Court at Chester retained an extensive jurisdiction in equity which largely excluded Chancery writs from the county.[4] Similarly the Court of Great Sessions retained an exclusive cognizance of all crown pleas and common law suits within Cheshire under its chief justice and puisne, assisted by a large permanant staff. One of the functions of this court was to sit twice a year as a court of assize. Whereas throughout most of the kingdom the royal judges from the three Westminster courts (together with the serjeants) set out to visit the shires and to perform political, administrative and propaganda tasks on behalf of the crown,[5] no judges tied closely to the central government ever visited Cheshire; the palatine justices frequently served for long periods and were clearly more closely bound to local interests than to national ones. The appointment of John Bradshaw to the post of chief justice of Chester in 1647 was particularly important. Bradshaw, a Cheshire man, was later president of the court that tried Charles I, and lord president of the Council of State, 1649-51, but became a leading opponent of the Protectorate. As chief justice, he played a vital role in the development of local government during the Interregnum. Many of the changes of this period involved the grand jury.

In some counties quarter sessions were always held in the county town; in others each session would be adjourned from one town to another for the convenience of those wishing to be heard within a reasonable distance of their homes. In Cheshire every session sat in just one place, but in the course of the year sessions would be held at

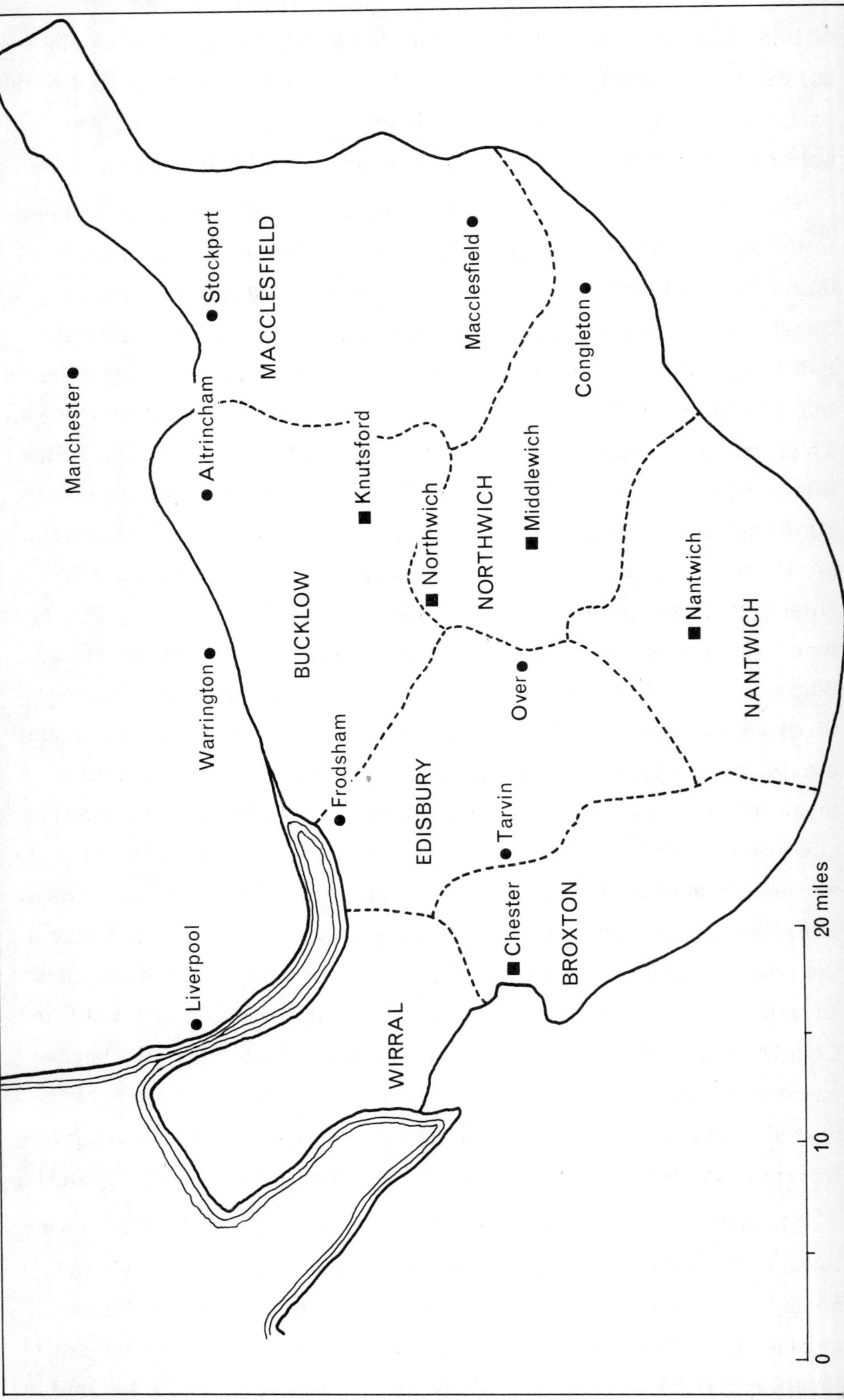

Cheshire: hundreds and sessions towns. (Hundred names are given in capitals; sessions towns are marked by a square, other market towns by a dot.)

four separate towns. The pattern was never completely settled, but for most of the period under review the general pattern was for Epiphany sessions to be held at Chester, Easter sessions at Knutsford, Midsummer at Nantwich, and Michaelmas at either Northwich or Middlewich. Every year sessions thus became easily accessible to all the inhabitants of the county at least once.

Finally, it is necessary to emphasize the general importance of the hundred as an administrative unit within Cheshire.[6] The justices of each division were meeting regularly in each of the seven hundreds from at least the 1590s and much of the financial and social policy of the Bench relied heavily on the effectiveness of hundredal organization.[7]

In the ensuing sections, this paper will deal with the selection of and official control over grand juries; with the social status of the jurors; with the nature of their duties, with particular reference to the role of the presentment in the work of local government; and with the growing functional and political independence of the grand jury during the Interregnum. It will conclude with an attempt to compare the pattern which has emerged with that evident in other counties.

PATTERNS OF ATTENDANCE

Eight juries were sworn every year in Cheshire after 1629 - one at every quarter session and two at each assize (the grand and second inquests).[8] After allowing for a few missing panels, we are left with a total of 222 panels from the years 1625-59.[9] Yet the total number of men sworn to these juries was only 609. The very first point to be made, then, is that jury service was not an occasional or unique duty; for many it was a regular and important part of their lives. Furthermore, these 609 men came from only 497 families, since fathers were frequently followed as jurors by their sons, or brothers by brothers. Even during these years several families were represented by as many as four or five members.[10]

Taking the group as a whole, each juror served on an average of almost exactly six juries (5.97), but many served far more than this;

30 men served more then 20 times, ten more than 30 times, four 40 times or more. Most prominent of all were Philip Antrobus of Over Peover, who was sworn to 49 juries both at quarter sessions and assizes, and William Tomlinson of Wareton who sat 48 times. In the 17 years before his death in 1643, Humphrey Page of Yardshaw had served on 40 juries. These figures are a little misleading, however. They relate to an artificial period, 1625-59; many men had already served on juries for many years before the accession of Charles I or were to do so in the years after the Restoration. If we enquired how many of the men who served at any time during the years 1625-59 served, for example, 20 times or more during their lives, the number would rise from 30 to more than 70.[11]

Furthermore, this does not reveal the full burden of jury service, since the sheriff impanelled and summoned for jury service far more men than were ever sworn. Over 100 men were required to appear on at least 20 occasions during these years. In fact less than half of those summoned at any given session were actually sworn. Many made numerous wasted journeys, like Richard Bruch of Mobberley who sat on only six of the 21 occasions on which he was summoned. Even Philip Antrobus was not sworn on 15 occasions, being occasionally left out even after he had served on over 40 juries. It was not always the most senior men who were actually sworn.

There was, then, a semi-permanent core of grand jurymen who provided an important element of continuity to the system. Men like Humphrey Page, who sat on considerably more than one-third of all quarter sessions grand juries in the period 1625-42, attended more regularly than all but two of the justices of the peace themselves.

Some men were specialist jurymen at particular locations. Randle Grafton of Worleston was impanelled every year at the Midsummer sessions at Nantwich from 1617 to 1651. The same is true of assizes; George Bostock served on 27 of the 30 grand inquests between 1627 and 1642; John Edwards had a similar record as foreman of the second inquest in the years after 1631.

In marked contrast to many other counties, in Cheshire jury service both at assizes and quarter sessions was performed by the same men. 66 per cent of those who served on assize juries also served on quarter session juries; a further 12 per cent were impanelled but not sworn at quarter sessions.

Equally, there was no sense of graduation. Most men who served regularly would be sworn at one or the other indiscriminately. In a random sample of 100, it was found that 42 first served on a quarter session jury, 33 on an assize second inquest, and 25 on an assize grand inquest. Not much can be made of the differences.

It has been shown that juries at quarter sessions and assizes were complementary in membership and that many jurors served regularly. But what of it? Does this imply a deliberate belief in the importance of continuity and experience, or is it simply the laziness of local officials in continually selecting the same men? Direct evidence is lacking, but there are indications that great care was taken in the selection of particular jury panels.

A fortnight before each session, the clerk of the peace instructed the sheriff to impanel a sufficient number of freeholders from whom the jury was to be selected.[12] Although by statute the number impanelled should have been 24, this provision was interpreted loosely. At quarter sessions from 1625 to 1642, for example, sheriffs tended to impanel between 24 and 40 freeholders, while for assizes the number was greater, separate panels of between 40 and 60 being chosen for both the grand and second inquest. After 1646, the size of panels tended to rise, in the case of quarter sessions to a maximum of 50, in the case of assizes to 70 or even 90. The number actually sworn also tended to rise, from between 13 and 17 in the years 1625-42 to 21 or more after 1646,[13] but this hardly accounts for the scale of increase in the size of panels. Since the records frequently reveal the names of those who failed to appear (and with fines of between 20 and 40 shillings for non-attendance there were strong incentives to appear), and since these records suggest an absentee-rate of around 10 per cent, the size of the panels cannot have been necessitated by the difficulty of finding a quorum on the day.[14] Part of the explanation may have been the requirement that a roughly equal number be summoned from each hundred; but it is difficult to escape the conclusion that judges sought panels which would allow them some freedom of choice in selecting juries weighted with men from those parts of the county about which, in any given circumstances, they might require the greatest amount of information.

An examination of individual panels gives clearer evidence of the extent to which care was taken in the selection of juries. No two panels appear to have been completely the same. Indeed, no two consecutive quarter session panels appear to have contained more than 40 per cent of the same names, and no two consecutive panels for sessions in the same town contained more than 60 per cent of the same men. Care was constantly taken to ensure a degree of variety as well as a degree of continuity. Every jury during this period contained a clear majority of men who had previous experience of grand jury service. This holds true even of those juries which sat in the sessions immediately after the disruptions of the Civil War. For example, at the first post-war sessions, at Knutsford in October 1645, the jury comprised nine experienced jurors, three men related closely to pre-war jurors, and three newcomers. Taking the years 1645-8 as a whole, almost 70 per cent of all those sworn had had previous experience. This figure almost exactly matches that for an earlier and more settled period. Of those who served in the years 1628-30, 71 per cent had had previous jury experience in the years before 1625.[15]

On the other hand, only one in six of all juries consisted entirely of men with previous jury experience. Well over half contained between two and four newcomers and very few appear to have contained more than six. In most years from 1633 to 1656[16] between 16 and 24 new men were introduced (i.e., two or three in each jury). Only in 1648 did the average rise to four per jury (still less than one-quarter of those sworn on each occasion). This represents a deliberate policy of the Bench, since there were always enough experienced men on every panel to form a jury. In October 1655, for example, 55 of the 85 men on the assize panel and 30 of the 36 on the quarter session panel were experienced. Yet three of the 17 sworn at the assize and two of the 15 sworn at the quarter session possessed no previous jury experience.

Both the judges and the jurymen were regularly concerned to ensure that the freeholders' book was kept up to date. John Bradshaw was particularly insistent on this point. In 1652, he even ordered the sheriff not to impanel the same men at successive sessions, and he later made special arrangements to spread the burden of service more widely in Macclesfield, the most distant of the hundreds from Chester. Juries also gave advice on selection. In October 1652 they presented that 'there are divers sufficient freeholders in the towne of Nantwich none of which were Returned nether have for manny yeares appeared to doe service for the County at the Assizes, whereby the excesse and disorders of the said towne might be made known and presented to this Court.'[17]

Sheriffs were instructed that men from every hundred were to be impanelled, but no such rule governed the choice of those actually sworn on to juries from these panels. Thus, while all assize juries were selected from panels containing an equal number from each division, those actually sworn normally came from only three or four hundreds. It is no surprise to find that in most cases a majority of the subsequent presentments referred to the same parts of the county. What matters is whether it was an effect deliberately sought by the justices. May they have chosen a majority from, say, Edisbury and Macclesfield, because they had reason to believe that there were serious unreported misdemeanours and administrative defaults in those areas which required particular attention? This question will be considered later, but it is worth noting here that this might go far towards explaining the large number of men impanelled for each hundred. It may also explain why the judges regularly caused some men to be sworn on to a jury who had not been on the sheriff's panel. The ensuing presentment can frequently be found to contain an item attributable to the knowledge of these men, whose presence may have been intended to ensure that the court could take official notice of a rumoured injustice. It should also be noted that over the period as a whole, a balance between the several hundreds was achieved; assize juries were not consistently drawn from some parts of the county rather than others. All the hundreds except Bucklow and Edisbury provided between 40 and 60 of the 410 men who served on assize juries between 1625 and 1659.[18] Furthermore, although a particular jury at assizes might contain concentrations of men from one or two divisions of the county, it was very unusual for less than four hundreds to be represented on any assize jury. Frequently all seven would be represented. It is significant, moreover, that newcomers were most usually to be found within the larger groupings; it is most unusual for a hitherto untried juror to be the sole representative of his hundred. And since there were two juries of presentment at every assize after 1629, it usually happened that a concentration from particular divisions in the grand inquest would be balanced by a different pattern in the second inquest.

Fairly standardized arrangements existed at each of the five quarter session towns. Whenever sessions were held at Chester a fairly even representation of Wirral, Edisbury, and Broxton men was sworn; at Knutsford a clear majority usually came from Bucklow hundred, with a smaller number from Macclesfield and Northwich hundreds. At Middlewich and Northwich sessions most of the jurors came from Northwich, Edisbury, and Bucklow hundreds, usually with one or two from Macclesfield; and at Nantwich sessions the great majority came from Nantwich hundred, usually with a few from Broxton and Northwich.[19] Clearly the aim was that the presentments should concern largely the areas closest to the town where the session was being held. Similarly, I have shown elsewhere that many justices appeared only at those sessions closest to their own homes.[20] But this arrangement was not adopted for the convenience of prospective jurymen, for the panels from which the juries were chosen invariably contained the names of men from all seven hundreds who were then required to attend the court. From time to time men from other hundreds were indeed sworn. For example, 19 Bucklow men were sworn at one time or another to quarter session juries at Nantwich, although the great majority of all juries there came from the three southerly hundreds of the county. At least eight men served as quarter session jurors at all five session towns (Richard Whittingham of Over in Edisbury serving at least three times at each town), and at least 16 others served at four of the five towns. Once again, when these 'outsiders' were included in such juries, the probable explanation, borne out by the ensuing presentments, is that their inclusion was made in order that matters of which they had personal knowledge could be brought to the attention of the court.

Thus it can be argued that the composition of grand juries was carefully controlled and regulated by the county authorities, and prima facie that this indicates that the functions of grand jurymen were considered by the Bench to be of great importance.

THE STATUS OF THE JURORS

Thus far, the analysis has rested on fairly straightforward calculations; but any discussion of the social and economic background of the jurors is bound to be more controversial and inconclusive. The following discussion is made even more difficult by the lack of agreement amongst contemporaries about the qualification for service on juries of inquest. Lambarde, basing his opinion on statutes of 1419 and 1439, asserted that 'each juror of enditement and triall ought to have yerely value of five pounds', but others held that these statutes referred only to the county palatine of Lancaster.[21] It was also claimed that the statute of 27 Elizabeth c. 6 had increased the property qualification from 40 to 80 shillings freehold;[22] but this interpretation in turn appears to have been a misreading of a statute whose operative clauses related principally to juries impanelled in the provinces for service at Westminster (on writs of venire facias), and also to assize trial juries. At one point Dalton draws attention to this misrepresentation,[23] but elsewhere he implies that the qualification remained the 20-shilling freehold laid down in what (with uncharacteristic vagueness) he styles an 'ould statute'. With his usual eye for expediency, Dalton added that allowance has to be made for the subsequent change in monetary values.

Whatever the statutory requirements really were, it is clear that sixteenth- and seventeenth-century clerks and sheriffs differed widely in practice, and tended to follow local custom.[24] At any rate, the writs from both the clerks of the peace and the clerks of assize to the Cheshire sheriffs during this period instructed them simply to impanel 40-shilling freeholders.[25] This would, in fact, have made a very large number of men liable to jury service. An exhaustive recent survey has indicated that in practice about one in four of all adult males may have claimed the right to vote in early Stuart England;[26] this would suggest a figure of perhaps 4,000 nominal 40-shilling freeholders in Cheshire. Clearly the 500 families who actually served during this time formed only a fraction of the freeholder class. At first sight it is tempting to see the jurors as forming the most substantial members of this group. This is also suggested by the fact that all 500 families were regarded as gentry in the jury panels.[27] All but a handful were in fact styled 'gentleman'; a few were referred to as 'esquires'.

Furthermore, the fines exacted by the justices of the peace and judges from jurors who failed to appear at sessions suggest that an income well in excess of the minimum was expected. The fines - 20 or 40 shillings before 1645 and invariably 40 shillings after that date - were doubtless intended to be punitive, but the offence was hardly one grave enough to require the confiscation of a whole year's income.

Is it possible to give some indication of the income range of the jurymen without engaging in a long and dubious investigation of such sources as <u>inquisitiones post mortem</u>? The arguments against such an investigation are persuasive[28] but something may be gained from a study of two readily accessible sources.

First, there are the records of the commissions for distraint of knighthood issued by Charles I in the early 1630s. The commissioners, in accordance with a moribund statute, were instructed to list all those gentlemen with incomes of £40 a year or more who had failed to sue for knighthood on Charles's accession. By adding together the names in these lists with the known number of Cheshire knights from the early seventeenth century, it is possible to compile a list of exactly 250 families with incomes of £40 a year or more. It has been argued elsewhere that this commission appears to have been reasonably comprehensive and accurate, but in any case the main point can be clearly established. Of these 250 families, only 58 were sworn to grand juries in the years 1625-59. This represents only 12 per cent of the total number of jurymen, or 22 per cent of all those who served in the years most closely relevant to the commission (1627-37). Equally suggestive is the fact that all 58 compounded at the minimum rate (£10), which, in view of more general evidence, can be taken to indicate that none of them had incomes of more than £100 per annum.[29]

The second source, the extensive sequestration and composition records for Cheshire, is less reliable. Yet it confirms the picture already sketched out. While 30 grand jurymen compounded for delinquency,[30] at least 36 others were discharged from sequestration as possessing personal estates of under £200 capital value. Making the reasonable assumption that the royalist group is a typical cross-section of the whole, this would certainly suggest that a majority of the grand jurymen had incomes of not much more than £10 per annum. Of the 30 who compounded, ten paid fines which suggest a revenue of between £10 and £40 a year, 16 paid fines representing between £40 and £100 pounds a year, and four incomes in excess of that.[31]

Confirmation of the view that many of the grand jurymen must have had small incomes is provided by the fact that members of 17 families from the village of Mobberley served on grand juries in the years 1625-59. All were gentlemen-freeholders in a manor which had been broken up at the dissolution of the monasteries. The excellent Bucklow sequestration records indicate that six of these families also held messuages in other townships, but the other 11 do not appear to have done so. Similarly, 12 gentlemen-freeholder families from Latchford township served on juries during these years.

A consistent picture thus appears. The jurors came from a broad spectrum of middling freeholders with incomes and status well below that of the magisterial class. Of the 250 families with incomes of £40 a year indicated by the distraint of knighthood records, 58 families served on juries and a further 70 formed the magisterial class.[32] Between these two groups came a group of 120 families, many of whom were forced to compound at above the minimum rate, but who were not expected to serve on juries. The papers of the Committee for Compounding with Delinquents point to a similar conclusion. Excluding former magistrates and former jurymen, there remains a group of 68 gentry families who compounded for their estates, the great majority of them for incomes of more than £100 a year. The average income of this group was more than double that of the jurymen-compounders but well below that for the magistrate-compounders. It appears undeniable that there were a great many gentry families who were both unable to aspire to the Bench and the shrievalty and yet were considered too substantial to be required to perform jury service. This group comprised a majority of the Cheshire 'esquires'.

The disparate sources, shaky as they are, all point in one direction. The jurymen represent the lowest section of the gentry. Yet despite the fact that a large number can have had incomes of barely £10 a year, they were all styled 'gentleman'. Granted the existence of a large number of Cheshire yeomen,[33] these implausible gentry raise important problems of definition. Only five of the grand jury families were included in the Heralds' Visitations, taken by many historians as the principal test of gentility. Equally, use of sequestration and other records would quickly establish that many families styled as yeomen could claim incomes well in excess of these very minor gentry. It seems that attempts to explain gentility in economic terms are totally inadequate. Equally, it seems difficult to believe that the very minor gentry were set apart from the yeomanry by differences in life-style. They must have had more in common with the yeomanry than with the squirearchy. Yet here, in the grand jury lists, is an official source which stubbornly attributes gentility to all the jurymen.[34] It might be suggested, tentatively, that selection for jury service in some cases actually conferred the status of gentility, and that what set the mere gentleman apart from the yeoman was an acknowledgment by the community that he was capable of upholding a responsible role in his county. Was there, in the lower reaches of the gentry, a gentility of social function? If so, the lack of serious complaints from those called upon to perform jury service is not surprising. It appears to have been the only job in the middling and minor levels of local government which Cheshire men made little effort to avoid, despite the fact that it required at least three days' absence from home and work. True, the jurors were offered hospitality each evening in one of the better inns at the session town, but this can hardly have been the main attraction of service on the jury.[35]

Despite the difficulties of the source material, then, it can be argued that grand jurymen came from a coherent social group, the middling freeholders. They were not those immediately below the magisterial class in status, and they were separated from the humbler freeholders less by wealth than by official recognition of their capacity to perform disinterested tasks for the good of the local community. This impression is also confirmed by the fact that it was from precisely the same groups that other officials of middling importance were drawn.

The most important of these other officials were the head constables, two of whom served at any time in each hundred. Responsible for a wide range of fiscal and judicial duties, they were a vital link in the enforcement of the social and economic orders prescribed by Parliament, Privy Council or justices of the peace. Between 1625 and 1659, 266 men served as head constables. Almost two-thirds also served as grand jurymen, the great majority before they served as head constables. Of the 50 most active jurymen, 32 also served as head constables, usually fairly early on in their careers.[36]

Perhaps it would be admissible to note here that, in Cheshire at least, trial juries were drawn from exactly the same group as grand juries. The point is worth making because it has been commonly assumed that trial juries comprised men of lower status. Unfortunately, panels listing petty jurymen survive only for the assizes, but these lists provide a total of 289 men sworn during the period 1625-59. Of these, 229 (79 per cent) also served on grand juries. With about six assize petty juries being sworn each year, service on these juries was often more regular even than service on grand juries.[37] In a sample of 50, over three-quarters (39) served first on a grand jury and then on a petty jury, which suggests that experience of finding indictments was considered a desirable background to the actual trial of offenders.

The grand jurymen were a coherent body of men, experienced in the work expected of them, and, frequently, in the problems on which they were expected to advise the court. In the second half of this study I shall turn from the examination of the jurors themselves to look at their actual role in the workings of local government.

THE EVOLUTION OF THE GRAND JURY

The grand jury system evolved slowly, and its powers were established as much by convention as by statute.[38] By the Assize of Clarendon a jury impanelled by the sheriff was to 'present' to the King's justices all those who by 'reputation' had committed murders and robberies, who were then put to trial either by ordeal or before men who knew the circumstances of the alleged crime. Jurors were in fact crucial to the detection rather than the trial of offenders. But gradually and largely by custom their duties in this respect changed. By about 1360 the first stage in presenting criminals had been taken over in practice by the serjeants or justices of the peace. Complaints from neighbours about breaches in the law were received by the justices, who took written statements or examinations of the accused and the witnesses and summarized the charges in a bill. At the sessions all bills were submitted to the grand jury who found them true or insufficient (<u>'ignoramus'</u>). True bills were then held to constitute an indictment and the accused proceeded to trial either before his neighbours, or, increasingly, before a jury of 12 representing the community as a whole. But although the 'indictment' became a central feature of the criminal process, grand juries retained a distinct right to present on their own knowledge. In fact, the presentment increasingly evolved into a device for drawing attention primarily to administrative defaults rather than to criminal acts. It lost most of its formal judicial status and came to serve as a basis for a court order rather than as an alternative form of indictment. In so doing, it greatly increased the effectiveness and importance of the grand jury within the framework of local government.

This paper cannot concern itself with indictments. Despite the existence of both bills (many but not all with grand jury 'billa vera' or 'ignoramus' findings at their feet) and indictment summary books, it is impossible to make much of them. The decision is too often uncertain and there are too many discrepancies between bills and indictment books for accurate statistics to be compiled. From samples taken, it seems that grand juries rejected an absolute minimum of 8 per cent of all bills, which is enough to show that their assent was far from automatic. Indeed, the percentage is likely to have been much higher. However, it has proved impossible to take this point further. There is no evidence to support the view that juries were particularly likely to dismiss bills in capital cases.

SWEARING AND CHARGING

The first morning of the assize or quarter session was spent on lengthy formalities. Amongst the first of these was the swearing of the grand jury. The sheriff delivered a copy of his panel to the clerk who then required the crier to call out the names of all those in the panel 'to answer your names... and save your fines'. This he did twice. If a sufficient number had appeared, the court proceeded to select the jury; otherwise any freeholder present in court could be summoned to make up the numbers. Indeed, 'if the Court dislike any of the names returned in the Pannel, and command the sheriff to add, alter or diminish any of them, he shall forthwith do the same and put in others, according to the discretion of the Justices.' Once the selection had been made, one of their number took the oath for them, being charged by the marshall:

> You as Foreman of this Inquest, for the body of this County of H. you shall diligently enquire, and a true presentment make of all such matters and things as shall be given you in charge: the Kings

> Majestys Counsel, your fellows, and your own you shall keep secret, you shall present no man for envy, hatred or malice, neither shall you leave any man unpresented for love, fear, favour or affection, or hope of reward, but you shall present things truely as they come to your knowledge according to the best of your understanding; so help you God.

The others were sworn as follows, three at a time: 'The same oath which your Foreman hath promised to observe and keep on his part, you and every of you do promise to observe and keep your parts; so help you God.' The jury then remained seated in court until the rest of the routine business was over.[39] The chief justice (at assizes) or a senior justice of the peace (at quarter sessions) then delivered the charge.

Grand jury charges followed no set pattern. The legal handbooks urged those delivering the charge to concentrate on those areas of the criminal law with which the jury would be most concerned. But in practice judges and justices appear to have been concerned to teach juries how to present rather than how to indict. Thus Professor Cockburn has shown how assize judges, acting on instructions from the law officers of the crown, concentrated in their charges on those aspects of social, economic and religious policy which the Privy Council felt were being neglected. There is some ground for thinking, indeed, that assize charges were directed more at the justices of the peace than at the jurors.[40]

Few grand jury charges have survived for Cheshire during our period, and, unhappily none at all from assizes. From quarter sessions we possess a whole series delivered by Sir Peter Leycester immediately after the Restoration and two delivered by Sir Richard Grosvenor in 1625.

Leycester's are a curious series.[41] They were essentially elegant homilies on the nature of English law and hardly touched on the work of the grand jury. His first charge began by defining the various kinds of criminal offence (treasons, felonies, misprisions, praemunires and 'other Finable offences against the Public Peace') and continued with an analysis of the various offences under each of these headings. Significantly this treatment required several charges at different sessions to complete, the initial charge in October 1660 treating only treasons and felonies, the other categories being reserved for later occasions. This in itself is important evidence of the extent to which Leycester expected to address the same men each time. What is surprising is not so much his concentration on the legal definition of each category of offence as his very general treatment of the criminal process. For example, he listed suitable penalties for every offence, giving, en passant, an unpleasantly full account of the punishment for treason. He also explained in great detail the extent and nature of benefit of clergy, which was of no relevance to the work of the jury. The overwhelming impression is that Leycester was directing his remarks mainly at his fellow justices, many of whom, in the years after 1660, were young and inexperienced former royalists.

By comparison, Sir Richard Grosvenor directed himself to the immediate worries and concerns of the jurymen themselves. Although he listed the criminal offences with which they were expected to deal, he was at pains to explain the importance of the juries' contribution to the legal process. He stressed the practical benefits which would accrue to them personally and to the community as a whole if they performed their duties fully: 'You (Gentlemen) are the persons who are at this tyme trusted (as the eyes of yor Countrey) to spye out and bringe such to their deserved punishment.' He stressed that 'the profitt will rebound both to yourselves and country if acted conscionably.' His second charge similarly aimed at persuading them not to give way to the wishes of great men or of their neighbours, nor to allow 'foolish pitty' to stand between them and their duty. Furthermore, his treatment of felonies and misdemeanours was concerned not simply with expounding the law, but also with pointing out the social consequences of the neglect of particular laws. In each case he drew attention to particular areas of neglect: 'you are also to inquire if watch and ward have beene duely kept according to the lawe. If this were better looked to, we should not bee pestered with such swarmes of rogues from all partes as wee are. But till some constable be made a severe example for neglecting his duety in this respect, wee shall find noe reformacon.'[42]

The importance of Grosvenor's charges was that they gave the jury a great sense of their own responsibility. Whereas Leycester's charges were brilliant intellectual dissertations concerned with making sense of a mass of precedent and statute, Grosvenor's aim was to give the jurors a sense of involvement and an incentive to act. In the next section we shall see how they responded to his challenge.

PRESENTMENTS

The presentment was the most flexible of the powers possessed by the grand jury. However, the great majority of all presentments were purely routine and repetitive. They ought also to have been unnecessary, for presentment was only one of several ways in which the justices' attention could be drawn to defaults and abuses in county government.

Every month, the justices met in their hundreds to carry out routine administrative tasks. Many of these were simple enough; men who sought licences to open alehouses or to act as carriers of grain would appear for consideration. Other duties required information to be provided by lesser officials. The justices had to confirm certain village appointments, notably the overseers of the poor and the surveyors of the highways; and they had to listen to appeals by those seeking to avoid service as petty constables. They were also responsible for reviewing parish poor rates. But over and above this they received 'presentments' both from the head constables and from the petty or village constables. None of these presentments have survived, so that comparison is difficult, but it seems probable that a majority of the presentments made by the grand juries at quarter sessions and assizes dealt with matters which ought properly to have been presented at monthly meetings. In this respect the return of the head constables of Wirral to the assize grand jury in April 1656 is highly revealing. They reported that 'we have sent all defaults before the justices att their monthly meetings and have nothing to present.'[43] If the system had worked well, there would have been few presentments to be made at quarter sessions or assizes.

A second alternative to formal presentment by jury was provided by the right of the individuals or groups to petition the justices or judges at sessions. On average 18 such petitions survive in each quarter sessions file for the years 1625-42, 38 in each for the years 1645-59. They range widely, but a majority concerned the operation of the poor laws, the upkeep of bridges and the erection of cottages on waste land. Significantly these are all matters not normally covered by the grand jury. Such petitions were sufficient to empower the court to proceed to make a formal order.

The grand jury, then, was only one of the means by which the county authorities took cognizance of defaults and abuses. But ultimately it was the most important. Petitions were often incoherent or confused, and local officials often sought to cover up their own failings. The grand jury alone could, and did, present corruption and error within the local government system.

The work of the grand jury was generally spread over two days. On the first it spent the morning being called, sworn and charged; it spent the afternoon reading and finding the indictments. It turned to presentments on the second morning. Here again, as with indictments, it was given material to work with. For on the first afternoon, while the jury was out considering the bills, the justices formally received presentments handed in by a wide range of local government agents. It was the duty of every head constable to make a return to the court of all defaults known to him. He could either send in lists as he received them from his petty constables or make a digest of such returns. Furthermore, churchwardens were empowered to present recusants resident in their parish. The justices of each division could also make a presentment based on information received at their hundredal meetings. In practice they appear to have exercised this right only occasionally, usually in order to present the names of recusants, or lists of alehouses they wished to suppress. These presentments were received but not immediately accepted by the court. Instead they were handed over to the grand jury, or in the case of assizes divided between the grand and second inquests. As in the case of indictments the court did not proceed until the jury had accepted and endorsed these presentments as 'true bills'.

The system was not particularly effective. Time after time the head constables made the simple return that 'they have nothing to present', and increasingly they made no return at all. Grand juries responded by themselves presenting the head constables for neglect of duty. For example, in March 1652, the grand jury at the assizes reported that 'wee present all the head constables in our county who have not brought in there presentments whereby we are disinabled to present many misdemeanours in our county excepting Bucklow hundred and Edisbury hundred both which have appeared.'[44]

A year later John Bradshaw revised procedures to ensure a fuller flow of presentments from these official sources. He ordered that

> For the future all the high constables within this county of Chester from tyme to tyme successively doe at least a moneth before every great sessions to bee houlden for the said county send forth their warrants to the petty constables of the severall townshippes within their respective hundreds thereby requiringe them to appeare before them att such dayes and places as the said high constables shall limitt and prefixe them to bee at least a weeke before every such sessions to bring with them true and perfect presentments in writeinge of all such offences and misdemeanours as have beene donne and comitted within their severall constablewickes since the then last sessions and that the said high constables doe receave from them all such presentments and deliver the same into the Court of Great Sessions together with further presentmente from their own knowledge.[45]

But these presentments by minor officials were only the starting point for the grand jury. Having viewed and discussed the various items laid before them from these official sources, they added items of their own. For example, a unique second inquest presentment of April 1655 which named the source of each of the items reveals that a majority of them arose from the personal knowledge of members of the jury.[46] This kind of personal knowledge was the jury's most important contribution to local government. If the jury had not been able to make presentments over and above, and frequently against, other officials, the court would have remained ignorant of, and powerless to deal with, some of the most intransigent problems of county government.

The power of the jury was, of course, open to abuse. It gave the jurors an opportunity to settle private scores or gain personal advantage. Thus in October 1633 the grand jury at quarter sessions presented Thomas Barker of Over, tanner, for 'withdrawing a servant' of Raphe Maddock of Over, a member of the jury.[47] In 1640 the assize grand inquest presented a neighbour of Paul Wynington, juror, for a serious trespass in regularly crossing Wynington's private land to take his cart to Warrington, and with stealing the locks with which the gates were secured. This presentment was clearly just one move in a complex local feud.[48] In 1649 at least two of the items in the second inquest's presentment were of a similar nature: the theft of a saddle from Ralph Whittingham's barn, and a charge of assault against the constable of Hulme Walfield, were in each case clearly due to the initiative of jurymen who had themselves suffered from the activities of those presented.[49] But such items did not form more than a small minority of all presentments.

For reasons which are given below, it is impossible to set forth the incidence of various kinds of presentments in a statistical form.[50] But the overall picture is quite clear. Far and away the most frequent sort of presentment is that concerned with the state of the county's highways. There is hardly a surviving presentment that does not contain a substantial list of officials or individuals who had failed to ensure that the highways were properly maintained. The majority of these were concerned with the failure of the surveyors of the highway to enforce the statutory communal work on the roads; but individuals responsible for making public ways unpassable by failing to scour their ditches or clip hedges, or by digging pits affecting the drainage of the highways, were also regularly presented. At least 600 such items appear in surviving quarter session presentments for these years, and the number at assizes may well be even higher. A similar group of presentments dealt with the collapse or dilapidation of bridges, though in these matters responsibility lay with the hundred rather than the parish.[51] The only other categories to appear with great regularity were, first, the presentment of officials - notably head constables and sheriff's bailiffs - either for neglect of their duty or for abuse of their position,[52] and second, the presentment of unnecessary, immoral or unlicensed alehouses.

Apart from these matters, presentments covered an enormous range of problems, only some of which can be safely categorized. Amongst those which recur from time to time are problems relating to the movement of corn (particularly those concerned with the activities of badgers and maltsters); the unauthorized erection of cottages; a wide range of local squabbles and feuds between neighbours which affected the community as a whole; problems associated with enclosure; and disputes arising out of the assessment and collection of local rates and taxes.

Many presentments, however, defy classification. For example, in 1628 Thomas Gleave of High Legh, butcher, was presented 'for keeping a masty[ff] dogg untyed which putteth his neighbours' children in fear'.[53] In 1647 the jury presented Thomas Cowper for 'making a dung-hill in a yard adioyning to the wall of Richard Acton's House, whereby the water issueing therfrom sinkes into his house to his great annoy-ance'.[54] In 1656, they presented Joseph Tovey 'for removinge flaggs from the belhouse in the parish of Davenham into the chancell belonging to the said church'.[55] In 1652 the grand jury at the assize presented 'Edmund Birch of Alvanley for makeinge a writinge importing to be a devorce betwene John Pickeringe and Catherin his wyfe.'[56]

In many of these cases it is far from clear what law, if any, had been broken. The grand jury was more concerned with social nuisance than non-observance of the law. On one occasion, in the course of a presentment, they went so far as to request that six named men from Bucklow and Edisbury hundreds be allowed to 'take soe much timber out of delinquents' lands as shall be necessary for the repayre of Acton bridge'.[57]

What is striking about the overwhelming majority of all present-ments is that they were not concerned with breaches of the criminal law, but with failures in local economic and social policy. They were not disguised indictments and few led to the formal trial of those charged with defaults. They performed a double function: they allowed the justices to make administrative orders restraining individuals from socially harmful or disruptive activities, and they provided evidence from which the Bench could adduce the need to issue new general orders or revise old ones. Where presentments appear to come closest to the criminal law, their intention was generally preventive rather than punitive. For example, where they presented people as common scolds or disordered persons, or where they drew attention to local feuds, the intention was not to bring those named before the court for actual offences, but to allow the court to take action to prevent future incidents. The justices' response to such presentments indicates that this was the intention; they either referred the dispute to a local justice of the peace to settle, or they bound over all concerned on recognizances to keep the peace or to be of good behaviour. Such action was intended to take the heat out of the situation.

It should also be said that there were some sorts of presentment which greatly increased or decreased in the course of the period. For example, in the 1620s and 1630s alehouses were only presented when they had become socially undesirable, usually because the licensee had permitted disorder. After 1645 the jury concerned itself with keeping the number of alehouses down on principle, arguing that the licensing of too many alehouses was itself both morally and economically damaging. Thus post-war grand juries would draw attention to villages where they felt the number of licensed alehouses should be cut down.[58]

Other groups of presentments were more prominent at some times than at others. Thus the late 1620s saw a rash of presentments concerned with poaching and illegal sports, and also a campaign against those who offered houseroom to wanderers who could thereby establish a right to relief out of local rates. On the other hand, the presentment of recusants became far more regular and numerous in the years after 1640.[59] The breakdown of church courts after 1642, and the failure of Parliament to provide adequate machinery for the maintenance of ecclesiastical discipline, were partially offset by the grand jury's assumption of the right to present matters relating to the effectiveness of the clergy or the upkeep of parish churches. Several ministers were reported for neglect of duty, like Zachary Taylor, who in 1648 was presented 'for not observing the dayes of humiliacon & thanksgiving'.[60] More common were presentments about unkempt churchyards or the failure of parishioners to repair damage to the churches themselves. The presentments also reveal the activities of sectaries, such as Ralph Stone and Richard Sale for 'disturbeinge... the mynister... in publique Ordenance upon the Lord's Day', and for telling him 'thou lyes and leades the people into blindness';[61] or John Peckal who was presented for 'absenting the church & denying the sabboth day and sayinge it must downe as the holy dayes'.[62] In general, however, such views, and above all problems relating to the collection of tithes, occur remarkably infrequently in the presentments. None the less, the extent to which grand juries and lay justices took over the functions of the old church courts is an unstudied and perhaps an important aspect of the ecclesiastical history of the period.

How important, then, was the grand jury's exercise of the right to make presentments? First of all, it filled out the duties performed rather perfunctorily by the head and petty constables, who were weighed down by a multiplicity of other tasks and were closely connected with a great many local interests. The selection of a grand jury tended to determine the geographical pattern of presentments. At the quarter sessions held in October 1655, for example, the pattern of presentments was as follows:

	Jurors	Presentments
Broxton	6	4
Wirral	5	10
Edisbury	2	2
Northwich	1	5
Macclesfield	1	3
Bucklow	0	0
Nantwich	0	0

The point to note is not only that there were no returns for those hundreds unrepresented on the jury, but that there were particularly important items from those two hundreds, Northwich and Macclesfield, not usually represented on juries at Chester.[63] Similarly, the grand jury at the assize held earlier in 1655 produced a list of presentments chiefly concerning Broxton and Bucklow, and was dominated by jurors from those hundreds.[64]

Sampling throughout the period has produced similar results. It seems, therefore, that this pattern was determined by the deliberate choice of jurors from particular hundreds. This view is strengthened by the fact that the great majority of all presentments came from the jurors themselves. Where comparison is possible, it is clear that the jury took the lists from the various officials and added far more items of their own than they had received. The fact that a heavy concentration of jurors from a given area - a single parish in some instances - was usually followed by important items relating to that area strongly suggests that the Bench had selected the jurors with such a consequence in mind. The grand jury can thus be seen as a flexible instrument through which attention could be focussed on any trouble spot.

But the grand jury had other uses. One of the major hazards to efficient local government at this time was the lack of an inspectorate. How were county governors to establish the effectiveness of their policies if the main sources of information were the head and petty constables whom immediate self-interest would lead to make inaccurate or equivocal reports? Similarly, there was no machinery for checking the work of the surveyors of the highway or the overseers of the poor whose accountability lay personally to the Bench: the head and petty constables could hardly be expected to oversee other people's duties when their standard complaint was that they were overworked themselves. At any rate, they did not perform such duties. The grand jury, on the other hand, was a body uncommitted to other administrative duties and its members were entrusted specifically with the task of producing a list of such defaults as they had observed in their own neighbourhood. It was thus in a position to undertake this task of oversight, and it repeatedly recorded complaints against the head constables, sheriffs' bailiffs and other agents of county government, against whose corruption or neglect action would not otherwise have been possible. For example, in October 1656 the jury at Knutsford quarter session 'present[ed] William Steele of Hale, Bayliffe, for being a seditious person and for raising needles suits and likewise being baylife contrary to the statute'.[65] Head constables were most frequently presented for abusing their position as tax assessors or for neglect in collecting county rates; bailiffs most usually for taking bribes, on occasion from prospective jurors seeking to escape the burdens of jury service. For example, in 1653 a grand jury at the assize presented 'Owen Brundred a Bayliffe for takeing money of James Rayneshawe gent that he might stay att home fro the Assizes att that tyme hee was restrayned in Lymme by reason of the plague'.[66]

The presentment of officials thus formed an important part of the business of the grand jury. In most years between 15 and 30 petty and high constables would be presented at quarter sessions alone, and in 1652 as many as 84 were presented.

Opening one of his addresses to the grand jury, Sir Richard Grosvenor said: 'I have observed in my tyme three mayne enemies which hinder the perfection of this service whereof the first is a feare to offend great men our superiors.'[67] There is no doubt that the interest of great men and powerful neighbours, even village opinion, frequently undermined the efforts, or more likely the wills, of minor officials, and such interests also powerfully influenced the grand jury. Yet the status of the jury, its size and the partial secrecy and anonymity of its deliberations, may have gone part of the way towards allowing it to act where the isolated official dared not proceed. Presentments such as the following made by a quarter session grand jury in July 1657 suggest that, unlike minor officials, it was unafraid of the most influential figures in the community:

> wee present [Lord Cholmondely who] hath raised the bancke or damm of the river of Weever next above his mills in Namptwich in the said county of Chester two foote (or thereabouts) higher than it was heretofore or of right ought to bee to the damage & prejudice of diverse persons and against the publiq peace...

> Wee...present that Peter Venables Barren of Kinderton with force & armes doth continue severall cottagers both in Hunsterson & Bridgemere to the number of six or thereabouts not haveing four acres of land thereunto laid to be therewith continually occupied contrary to the statute.[68]

It is impossible to indicate how much the existence of presentments affected the efficiency of local government. Despite the fear of being presented, petty and head constables continued to neglect their duty and abuse their authority; but would even more have done so had the grand jury not existed in the form that it did? In any case, the presentments comprised only a tiny fraction of all administrative defaults. Yet in a world struggling to come to terms with new concepts of governmental responsibility in the fields of social and economic policy, it might be argued that the grand jury played an important part in the transmission of necessary information from village to county level, information not otherwise available. Its virtues were its flexibility, its independence from other official duties, its corporate strength and experience. Furthermore, it is possible that just as no accused man could be tried until he had been formally indicted by the grand jury, so many administrative defaults could only be rectified when the court was formally requested to act by a jury presentment. In those areas where no statute had been violated, the powers of the justices to proceed were ambiguous and limited. It does not seem that they could act on the basis of personal knowledge or common reputation. For example, in relation to the ecclesiastical problems created by the collapse of the church courts, there is no evidence that the justices ever issued orders except in response to a presentment.

THE GROWTH OF GRAND JURY INDEPENDENCE

The presentment had a further function. It was partly on the basis of jury presentments that the justices formulated new general orders. For example, John Bradshaw's comprehensive decree revising the methods by which alehouses were licensed followed (as he pointed out) from a long series of specific objections to the old order presented by successive juries.[69] Sometimes the jury went further and specifically called attention not to individual defaults but to general problems for which they offered general remedies. It is clear, however, that this became a regular feature of their work only after the Civil War, and even then much more frequently at assizes than at quarter sessions. A simple example, where a general grievance was expressed but no remedy provided, can be found at the quarter session in October 1645: 'first wee presente the multitude of alehouses in our County, so farr as wee conceive them to bee a greate burden to the Comonwelthe, and do not sell ale and Beere accordinge to the statute.'[70] Similarly, a jury in 1657 presented 'the generall neglect of the pettye constables within this county of Chester for neglecting their dutie in punishing wandring rogues and beggars and makeing them passes to send them to the place of their birth or abode by reason whereof many places of the Cuntry are full of Idle persons & many time much harm [is] donne by filching & steeling'.[71]

At times these general presentments referred to matters not regularly treated by the jury in their specific items. Thus a presentment at the quarter session at Knutsford in October 1655 deals with a matter which appears never to have caught the jury's attention before: 'wee present the generall abuse in this county of the excessive rates of servants and labourers and handicraftsmen contrary to the forme of the statute in that case made and provided; and desire in the behalfe of the county that the justices of the peace would rate the same accordinge as the statute appoynte'.[72] Six months later, an assize jury expressed the view that there were inadequate controls over weights and measures[73] - another matter to which they had never given any earlier attention.

What is striking about this kind of presentment in the period after the Civil War, however, is first, that juries began to present deficiencies within the structure of local government, and second, that they presented matters which can only properly be described as political rather than administrative, and which would hitherto have been no part of their brief. What is really remarkable about this group of presentments is that the grand jury was prepared to criticize directly the justices of the peace themselves.

During the period 1648-58 assize juries several times presented the justices for allowing inadequate men to be appointed as constables.[74] They criticized the official slackness which allowed head constables to make no serious attempt to produce worthwhile presentments for them to scrutinize.[75] They also commented on the failure of the justices to hold regular monthly meetings in each hundred, 'to the great obstrucktion of Reformation... [and] to the greate discouragemente of Many people That have any Occasion to make theire addresses to the justices of peace in any case wherein one single justice of the peace cannot acte'.[76] They were particularly critical of the justices' failure to take up grand jury presentments which sought to limit the number of alehouses: 'we doe present the multiplycitie of Alehouses which notwithstanding our former complaints is little or nothing redressed'.[77] At other times they were quite specific: 'wee present the excessive number of alehouses throughout the whole countie and the Justices' neclect in suppressing the same, and suffering the assize of bread and ale to be broken'.[78]

Perhaps the most striking evidence of the changing role of the grand jury after the Civil War was its assertion of a right to suggest suitable candidates for inclusion in the commission of the peace itself. In April 1648, the second inquest at the assize presented the names of six men deemed suitable for inclusion in the quorum, 'in respect of [their] fidelitie to kinge, parliament and country'.[79] Later, in 1652, they presented 'the want of a Justice of the Peace in Broxon hundred, there being but one, to wyt Peter Dutton of Hatton, esq, and wee desire that Thomas Tanat of Broxon Esq may have commission to officiat with Mr Dutton'.[80] In this latter case they actually nominated the man at that moment acting as foreman of the grand inquest sitting next door. Of the six men nominated in 1648, five were included in a new commission issued by Parliament a few months later;[81] Tanat was included in the commission when it was next revised. It is very tempting to relate these nominations to the demand for justices of the peace to be chosen locally, a demand that was put forward in the Heads of the Proposals - the army's programme for a settlement with the king in the summer of 1647.[82] The existence of these Cheshire nominations might well suggest that the army was responding to a genuine call from the freeholder class for a greater say in local government. It can surely be argued that in seventeenth-century conditions, the parliamentary franchise was of less importance to the middling sort than was greater participation in local government. Grand jury presentments of suitable justices may form part of a pattern of events in Cheshire which would suggest that this is precisely what happened in the later 1640s.[83]

The presentments in which juries made frankly political demands can also be seen as assertions of a new-found independence. One of the clearest examples of this independence was the jury's presentment in April 1648 that the burden of fresh military levies on the county to fight the second civil war was too great.[84] Another was its presentment in 1656 that 'uppon the 20th August last past, at the tyme of the eleccon of the knights of the sayd county to serve in Parl. The Pole was demanded from Philipp Egerton Esq highe Sheriffe of the sayd County, for the cleeringe of the eleccons and that the same was not granted by the sayd Sheriffe Contrary to the forme of the Statute'.[85] This presentment followed an election in which all the leading justices had engineered a victory for their own candidates at the expense of John Bradshaw and Sir William Brereton, the old county radicals.[86] While Bradshaw, who presided at the assize, may have put the jury up to this act of defiance, Brereton saw the presentment as a vindication of his personal interest, not Bradshaw's.[87] In any case this was a fairly experienced jury with no more newcomers than usual, picked by the sheriff who was the object of its criticism.

The jury's independent intervention in politics can be seen even more clearly in its petitions, the last of its functions with which we are concerned in this paper. In this case also the initiative was seized by juries prepared to speak out for policies distinctively their own in the face of official county policy. Grand jury petitions had hitherto been most usually employed by county leaders to add authority to local demands for action from either king or Parliament. There is no doubt tha an endorsement by a grand jury - 'the body of the county' - conventionally increased the status of petitions. They conferred an authority which even the signatures of a majority of the justices could not match. However, there is equally no doubt that until after the Civil War petitions rarely originated with the jury themselves; rather the initiative was taken by the justices who then called on the jury to support them. At times, particularly during a prolonged political crisis such as that beginning in 1640, the jury might be caught between warring factions in the commission of the peace. At such times the power of a sheriff to select the jury panel could be of vital importance. One example recently published is the packing of Somerset grand juries in 1648 by the radical faction within the county so that the jury would support the policies of John Pyne and his men.[88] The general pattern for other counties is similar; the jury was required only to confirm or to endorse petitions drawn up by others.[89]

Most of the petitions of the Cheshire grand jury were of this kind. In 1641 and 1642 grand juries joined with the majority of active justices in attesting four petitions concerned with major political issues. The first, in July 1641, called for an end to the socially divisive policies of the Personal Rule, in particular Ship Money, and demanded a thorough investigation of the activities of the sheriff, Sir Thomas Powell, in order that his illegal acts could be presented to parliament for redress. This represented the general consensus of county opinion on the subject: amongst the fiercest opponents of Ship Money were many future local Royalist leaders.[90]

The remaining petitions were all intended to lower the political temperature both locally and nationally. One was intended to put the case for moderation in ecclesiastical reform. Another was intended to persuade the king not to go to Ireland in person to quell the rebellion, a request couched in studiously moderate language and based on non-partisan arguments. The third was an expression of the county's inability to choose between king and Parliament, and a defence of its intended neutrality.[91] In all these cases the grand jury was just one of the groups signing the petition, although their endorsement was given prominence in each case.

However, grand jury petitions were comparatively rare before 1640. None was drawn up, for example, to support the county's case against the city of Chester during a fierce dispute over the distribution of Ship Money between shire and city in 1635-7.[92] Indeed, grand jury petitions appear to have been used regularly only after 1645, and then mostly in connection with essentially local matters. For example, in 1646 a jury at quarter sessions petitioned that the lack of supervision over wastelands in the county had created a series of problems connected with the unauthorized erection of cottages and shacks.[93] A petition of 1652 called for the full restoration of the Chester palatine jurisdictions,[94] while in 1658 an assize jury petitioned for the burden of jury service to be spread more widely since some regular jurors felt themselves to be overworked.[95] On several occasions the grand jury issued what were in effect public declarations of the county's loyalty to the existing government. For example, in 1652 the justices and grand jury together petitioned that they did 'from their hearts abhor and detest all designs tending to create New Troubles; and do bless God for the happy discovery of them and especially of that lately hatched in these Northern parts'. They even went on to congratulate the Rump on its just policies, but their enthusiasm was tempered by a demand for recruiter elections and a settled local court for probate of wills.[96] Similarly in April 1655 the justices and juries joined together to sing the praises of the Protectorate and to denounce all royalist plots.[97]

Petitions of this kind were no different from those promoted by the juries at the instigation of the gentry before the war. But there were a few which reveal the grand jury at work independently of the justices and again, at times, sharply critical of them. When a group of parishes in Macclesfield hundred petitioned against the extent of local mobilization during the second civil war, and the necessity of sending Cheshire troops into Wales, their ideas were taken up and endorsed by both the grand and second inquest. Yet those very soldiers had been recruited by militia commissioners who included all those active justices who were to receive and consider the petitions.[98] Similarly in 1651 all the grand inquest and all but one of the second inquest joined together to denounce the activities of the excise commissioners. They complained in particular that the commissioners had turned the excise into a direct tax, employing the usual county rating lists to levy sums in fixed proportion from each village rather then levying it on each individual's consumption of excised goods.[99] Again, there is no evidence that the justices themselves felt this to be a grievance. They offered no remedy, which they would surely have done, had the petition been instigated by them.

The clearest example of this growing independence of the grand jury, however, was the great attack on the deputy lieutenants mounted at the assize in October 1648.[100] Almost all the active justices in 1648 were also deputy lieutenants, and the subsidiary themes of the petition, particularly its attack on tithes, rule out the possibility that it was the work of moderates in the commission. The main charge was unequivocal:

> first wee present unto yor Lordships that wee have for diverse yeares last past and yet doe lye under an Arbitrary and unlimited power exercised by most of the Deputy Lieftenants of this County in their taxeing and imposeing greate burthens and payments upon us in the name of Mizes (wherein they themselves beare the leaste if any share at all with us) and in leavying the same upon our estates by distress without any Act or Ordinance of Parliament enabling or directing them thereunto and in particuler wee present the said Deputy Lieftenants assessing of Fower mizes. . . which tends to the losse of our propertye as freeborne Englishmen, and is directly against the Liberty of the Subject and the Law of the Land for which wee have lately and ever will ingage our lives and estates.

The language of this petition, together with the objects and preoccupations of the other independent jury petitions of the period, points quite clearly to the emergence of a distinct self-consciousness amongst the freeholders of the county. There is no reason to doubt that these petitions reflected the views of the jurors themselves and of their peers; the grand jury was no longer a cypher in county politics.

THE GRAND JURY AND THE GREAT REBELLION

Grand juries in the years after 1645 were far more self-confident and assertive than hitherto. Yet there was no change in patterns of membership or in the social status of those selected. Possibly changes on the Bench itself, which brought in justices with social origins closer to those of the jurors, help to explain this tendency, but the reasons surely lie deeper than this.[101] What is really surprising, however, is that the radical tendencies of post-war juries came from men whose political backgrounds were frequently Royalist.

It was noted earlier that there was a surprising degree of continuity between pre- and post-war juries.[102] The juries at quarter sessions between 1645 and 1648 contained a percentage of experienced men similar to that for the years 1628-30. Of those who sat between 1635 and 1642, 65 per cent served again after the Civil War, whilst a further 14 per cent were succeeded by their brothers or sons. This is a rather larger percentage than those who served between 1618 and 1625 and again after 1628. It is also slightly higher than the rate of continuity between the Protectorate and the Restoration. Clearly the freeholders' book was purged neither in 1645 nor in 1660. The list of grand jurors sequestered as delinquents during the Civil War[103] provides even more striking evidence of continuity; 30 of them served personally on juries in the years after 1645, while eight were represented by their sons or brothers. 71 per cent of all Royalist jury families continued to serve, a figure no different from that of the pre-war group as a whole.

In the course of the 1650s, sheriffs included more than 20 esquires, knights, and baronets in their assize jury panels. Some of them were former justices of the peace and all of them were of a status and wealth which placed them well above that of the usual jurymen. Every one of them had been sequestered as a delinquent. Their names invariably head the sheriff's return for their hundreds. Similarly five former justices of the peace who had been omitted from the commission of the peace for dissenting from the execution of the king were impanelled. The inclusion of these groups of men had great symbolic significance, although none of them was ever required to serve on the jury. It would seem to have been a gesture of goodwill from the new county authorities. Although banned by ordinance from serving in any position of trust in local or central government, the ex-royalists were being publicly associated with the interests and responsibilities of the community.[104]

CHESHIRE AND ELSEWHERE: SOME COMPARISONS

It remains to give some indication of the extent to which the pattern described above can be found in other counties. Not surprisingly, the conclusion will be that in some respects Cheshire was highly typical, in others unique.

To begin with, it is clear that in some counties the grand inquest at the assizes consisted largely or entirely of justices of the peace. But although this was the case in Oxfordshire and Sussex,[105] it was not so in Essex, Somerset, or Staffordshire.[106] However, Dr Cockburn, who has examined most surviving records, feels it safe to generalize that assize juries were made up of 'respected local freeholders... with a leavening of magistrates and lesser gentlemen'.[107]

More significant is the survival in many counties of minor juries of presentment. According to the Webbs, there were 'sets of jurymen from the several Hundreds, Liberties and Boroughs of the County... whose business it was... to present to the Court the delinquencies and derelictions of duty of their particular Hundreds or equivalent divisions in the same way as the Grand Jury did for the county as a whole.'[108] Lambarde discussed the operation of this system as it worked in Kent, where the hundredal juries were made up of petty constables. A similar system prevailed in Essex, but in Surrey the minor juries were drawn from the same panel as the grand jury. In Wiltshire the minor juries certainly contained men of lower status than the grand jury, but it is not clear whether they were parish officials. In Surrey the minor jury's presentments fulfilled the same role as those of the head constables in Cheshire; elsewhere the minor juries presented detailed and specific defaults while the grand jury concentrated on areas of general neglect.[109] But the system was not universal. In Hampshire it had almost ceased by 1600,[110] and in Staffordshire it appears never to have existed. Dr Burne's opinion is an interesting and probably correct one: 'it is worth noting that in counties where these juries are found...

the hundreds are numerous and the burden of jury service on the basis of hundreds altogether more grievous than in Staffordshire with its five hundreds.[111]

Cheshire was thus amongst the minority of counties which did not have hundredal juries, and was equally unusual in having a second inques at the assizes. However, once more it was not unique. Lincolnshire had a second jury made up of head constables 'for the ease of other free-holders',[112] while in Staffordshire two juries were drawn from the same panel and proceeded to divide the bills of indictment between them. It is even possible that the Staffordshire juries exchanged true bills, trying those whom the other jury had indicted.[113]

There is little evidence as to the regularity with which men were impanelled to juries. Dr Quintrell feels that in Essex grand jurymen 'usually served every few years', but he does not document the point.[114] Mr Willis-Bund asserts firmly that in Worcestershire the same men appeared 'again and again'.[115] Only Dr Burne has attempted even a rudimentary statistical analysis: having examined Staffordshire panels for the years 1586-91, he found that one man was included 18 times, and seven others ten times or more; but he reported no further findings.[116]

Most editors are less reluctant to generalize about the social status of grand jurymen. Once again their views are impressionistic and derivative from one another, but they are fairly specific. They fall into two groups. Except in those counties where assize juries were drawn from the upper gentry, the jurymen are said to come either from the middling gentry, or from the yeomanry and wealthy freeholders. The anonymous Office of the Clerk of Assize, probably based on the conventions of Lincoln, asserts that the jury should comprise 'the most sufficient freeholders in the County (who be not assigned Commissioners by the Commission of the Peace)'; and it has been claimed that this description applies to the men chosen at quarter sessions and assizes in Surrey, Staffordshire and Warwickshire.[117]

More typically, commentators have described the jurors as very minor gentlemen or else as wealthy yeomen. In Oxfordshire and Lancashire almost all appear to have been mere gentlemen; in Worcestershire gentlemen and yeomen; and in Hampshire 'lesser gentlemen and yeomen of significance'. In all these cases the same sort of men that sat on the Cheshire juries appears to be indicated.[118] In Essex and Lincolnshire the social position is even more clearly indicated by the fact that the juries consisted largely of head constables. In Sussex the grand jury was actually called the 'jury of constables'.[119]

In general, commentators have never got beyond simple descriptions of the functions of the grand juries. The essential similarity of indictments and presentments is frequently stressed, as is the monotonous and repetitious nature of most presentments. A few attempts have been made to demonstrate that grand juries threw out a high percentage of the bills, and that they were particularly lenient in certain sensitive areas; but most of the arguments lack conviction.[120] While the different sorts of presentments are frequently listed, often with entertaining examples, there has been little effort to estimate the role of the presentment in the general context of local government.[121] There are occasional references to the grand jury receiving draft presentments from the petty or head constables, but more usually the groundwork appears to have been done by the petty juries of presentment. In Worcestershire, however, there was a seemingly unique attempt to improve the flow of information: 'One of the duties of the chief constable was to ascertain from the constables of each parish any facts on which either the central government or the Court of Quarter Sessions required to be informed. For this purpose he sent A series of written questions to the constables and they were required to answer them.'[122]

But there is no doubt that grand juries elsewhere did possess one power never claimed in Cheshire:

> It was taken for granted that, when the County Gaol or the County Hall was out of repair, or the county bridges needed amendment, it was for the grand jury to initiate the proceedings by a formal presentment, before any action was taken by the Justices. In the case of bridges, the presentment by the Grand Jury had been recognised as a necessary preliminary by the statute of 22 Henry VIII

> c. 5 [1531]... There seemed much to be said for the view taken by some authorities that such a presentment by the Grand Jury was, strictly speaking, required, before the Justices could charge any payment on the county as a whole, or order each parish to contribute its quota of the amount.[123]

The requirement that the grand jury should consent to county rates was clearly widespread. The Webbs' examples all come from the north of England,[124] but other writers have noted its importance in counties such as Oxfordshire, Hampshire and Essex. In Essex, indeed, the grand jury fixed the composition rates for purveyance every Epiphany, and regulated wage rates every Easter.[125]

An excellent example of the scope and vitality of grand jury activity can be found in the notes and annals of the Worcestershire royalist, Henry Townshend of Elmley Lovell.[126] It is quite clear from the marginalia of his copy of The Complete Justice that most important administrative orders originated from grand jury action. For example, 'At Christmas Sessions at Worcester upon presentment of the Grand Jury it was consented to by the Court, that no alehouses shalbe allowed without certificat from ministers, officers and substantial persons of the parish'. This order of 1661, which went on to lay down further conditions, followed on from earlier county orders of 1634 and 1649.[127] In 1631, 'by the peticon of the Grand Jury... it is ordered that there be no making of mault within this county untill the next Generall Sessions, unles it be for provision of their own privat houses'.[128] In 1652 the jury ordered a full investigation of all weights and measures in the market towns of the county.[129] In 1661 a jury complained that 'the multitude of cottages erected during the tyme of the late warr to be a greate grievance', and the Bench ordered them all to be pulled down. At the same session the jury petitioned that 'their shalbe no order of... the Justices for churchwardens or overseers of poore to finde howseroom for any lusty young married people...yf yong men marry before they have howses... let them lye under an oke'.[130]

Examples of jury endorsement of county rates also appear frequently in Townshend's notes. In 1630 and 1647, for example, juries approved rates for the repair of the county gaol or the house of correction. (In 1633 they even approved a fee of £20 per annum to be paid to a minister, George Drummond, 'elected to teach and instruct the prisoners for the good of their soulls').[131] In 1651 the jury approved a county rate of £500 for 'findinge poore people... materialls to set them on work to releeve themselves'.[132] In 1643 they were even consulted before the royalist commissioners of array set about levying an assessment of £3,000 per month for the king's forces.[133] Throughout the Civil War the grand jury played a leading part in legitimating the expedients of the royalist leaders, and in campaigning to prevent the county from being brought under the control of either the High Command or of externally appointed military commanders. They fought to preserve county autonomy and local interests and both Prince Rupert and Prince Maurice were careful not to cross them.[134]

CONCLUSION

Dr Cockburn has a low opinion of grand juries; he sees them as subservient, ignorant and conservative. 'The overwhelming impression is of a group preoccupied with the familiar and predominantly uncontroversial details of county administration and everyday provincial life'.[135] In this paper I have tried to suggest that this understates their significance. The grand jury system was a vital part of the administrative machine upon whose smooth operation much of the efficiency of the court depended. To extend the metaphor, 'the Gentlemen of the Grand Jury are... the great or grand spring, the Primum Mobile of the Court, that gives motion to all the other wheels, their presentments being the key that opens and shuts the proceedings of the Court.'[136] It is vital to realize that magistrates and judges could only proceed through formalized channels, and that they required others to bring matters within their jurisdiction. In many cases this could only be performed by the grand jury. Hence the need to select men of experience and the importance attached to continuity. But in an age in which it was easy enough to formulate policy but extremely difficult to establish whether it was being enforced, or, if enforced, successful, there was great need for sources of information distinct from the agencies of hundred and village government. This duty too could be undertaken and partially fulfilled by the grand jury. During the great political crisis of the mid-seventeenth century, the jury, representing the interests of the numerous freeholders and tenant farmers, could serve as a focus for communal discontents. The rising independence of the juries, and their interest in so many issues during the Interregnum both reflects this and represents one aspect of a general growth of political consciousness in the middle orders of Cheshire society during this period.[137]

Ultimately, the argument returns to a phrase in the Privy Council letter with which we began: 'such persons are better acquainted with the comon grievance of the Countie, then Justices are'. Largely as a result of its distinctive pattern of settlement, Cheshire was, at this time, a county of secluded manor houses. Most of the justices of the peace would have known a lot about their tenants, but little about their neighbours or their neighbouring villages. They did not frequent the local alehouse, but stayed at home to entertain their relatives and other members of the county élite. A conscientious justice would certainly devote a lot of his time to his official duties, but the overwhelming impression is one of passivity; he waited for complainants to come to him. In any case, only a small number of justices sat regularly at quarter sessions or assizes; the average attendance at quarter sessions throughout the period was only six.

On the other hand, the substantial freeholders who comprised the grand juries were much closer to the pulse of community life. They wer men with essentially parochial interests and contacts, though often with lands in several townships in the area of their homes. Yet they were definitely 'gentry', and their freehold security and possible social aspirations might have set them slightly apart from the social pressures and the consensus of opinion in the community. They were habitués of th alehouse, and they farmed their own land. Above all, they were accepted by their fellows as 'gentlemen' for reasons which were not purely economic but seem to include recognition of a certain independence in their outlook and character.[138]

It is easy to overplay the distinction and to idealize the jurymen as trusty men of the soil. Yet the convention of grand jury responsibility ('the eyes of the country', 'the body of the county') was universally accepted. The belief that the jurymen were those per quos rei veritas melius sciri poterit was accepted by Lambarde and reflected in Grosvenor's charges and in judicial concern that the selection of a jury should be carefully controlled. The system could have been improved: there ought to have been more presentments, more attempt to formulate new social strategies to deal with persistent problems, more effort to ensure a flow of information to and from minor officials. Yet the justices did maintain a vigilant control over the recruitment and selection of juries. They did submit themselves to, and sometimes accept, the jury's criticisms of their work. Certainly they were not trying to turn the grand jury into what it eventually became, a clerical office for checking the wording of indictments. As a result, the seventeenth-century grand jury was more than an insignificant part of the pageantry and bureaucracy of the English criminal process. Without the grand jury system, such benevolent paternalism as early modern local government practised would have been less systematic, less informed and less effective.

NOTES

Note Places of publication are given only for works published outside the United Kingdom.

1. P.R.O., SP 14, vol. 190, item 44. I am indebted to John Cooper for providing me with a transcript of this document, and for drawing my attention to several others used in this paper.
2. See Appendix I.
3. Several figures are affected by the arbitrary period for which they are compiled. A majority served before 1625 or after 1659 as well. It is in order to be able to offer some perspective that a period within that covered by my researches is given full consideration.
4. See the article on the Chester Exchequer by W. J. Jones in Tudor Men and Institutions, ed. A. J. Slavin (1972), 123-70.
5. J. S. Cockburn, A History of English Assizes (1972), particularly chapter 3.
6. See map on p. 8.
7. For a fuller discussion of the administrative history of Cheshire in this period, see J. S. Morrill, Cheshire 1630-1660: County Government and Society during the English Revolution (1974), chapters 1 and 6.
8. Before 1629 only one grand jury was sworn at each assize. The fact that the term 'grand jury' was not actually used at assizes raises a problem of definition. The alternative title of this study would be 'juries of inquest', but this would confuse the issue in a different way, for technically it would have involved a study of juries returned at petty sessions to enquire into riots and forcible entry, and also 'juries returned before escheators or beffore Commissioners of Sewers or upon the Statute of Bankrupts, Coroners, clerks of the markett etc.' (M. Dalton, The Office and Authority of Sheriffs, 1662 edn, 392). In the circumstances the title 'grand juries' appears to create fewer ambiguities, since the term is (and was) loosely understood to include juries of inquest at both assizes and quarter sessions.
9. See Appendix I.
10. The term 'family' is here used in a narrow, nuclear sense, to include only those sons and brothers of former jurymen who had inherited the freehold. Cousinage and connections by marriage are discounted. 410 families are represented by one member, 69 by two members, 12 by three, five by four (the Dods of Saughall, Furnivals of Betchton, Leighs of Ollerton, Lownes of Hassall, Williamsons of Chowley) and one by five members (the Bennets of Willaston).
11. See Appendix II.
12. For the procedure, see the anonymous Office of the Clerk of Assize (1682), particularly 29-31.
13. An odd number was invariably sworn since grand juries proceeded by simple majority, not unanimity.
14. In any case, the justices were empowered to include in the jury men whom the sheriff had not impanelled.
15. It is not surprising to find that the same is true of the grand juries in the years after 1660.
16. See Appendix IId.
17. Freeholders' books have been too often cited as if they were electoral registers. It is, however, quite clear that they are really jury lists (i.e., a selection from amongst the 40-shilling freeholders). For example, John Bradshaw ordered the sheriff to remove from his book all those too old for jury service. Yet these men would retain their votes in parliamentary elections. For evidence that freeholders' books were

simply lists of jurymen, see Lincolnshire Quarter Sessions Minutes, 1674-1695, ed. S. A. Peyton (Lincolnshire Record Society, vol. 25, 1931), lxxi; for the paragraph above, see P.R.O., Chester 24/129 no. 2, unfoliated; Chester 24/129 no. 4, unfoliated; Chester 21/4, fos 265, 292; C.R.O., Quarter Sessions Book 9a, f. 87.

18. Bucklow and Edisbury exceptionally provided 83 and 71. The hundred of residence is uncertain in 36 cases.
19. See map on p. 8; Middlewich and Northwich are both in Northwich hundred.
20. Morrill, op.cit., 9.
21. W. Lambarde, Eirenarcha (1592 edn), 376-80.
22. Staffordshire Quarter Sessions Rolls, vol. 2, ed. S. A. H. Burne (William Salt Archaeological Society, 1930), xxx.
23. Dalton, op.cit., 403.
24. Ibid., 402
25. C.R.O., Q.J.F. 79 no. 3, f.1.
26. This estimate formed the conclusion of a paper on the franchise delivered to a graduate seminar in Oxford in Michaelmas term 1972 by Derek Hirst and can also be found in his now completed Cambridge Ph.D. thesis (1973), soon to be published by Cambridge University Press under the title The Representative of the People?
27. This is also true of the 300 or so families impanelled but never sworn to juries.
28. H. A. Lloyd, The Gentry of South West Wales, 1540-1640 (1968), 22-30.
29. Printed in a Miscellany volume of the Lancashire and Cheshire Record Society, vol. 12 (1885), 191-223.
30. For a list of these records and a discussion of the content, see Morrill, op.cit., chapters 3 and 5, passim, and the bibliography.
31. John and Richard Fletcher of Norley, father and son, compounded for a joint income of £150, John Kelsall of Wimbolds Trafford for an income of £120, two others for incomes of about £110.
32. Only those families included in the commission during the period 1603-42 have been included for this purpose. A further 20 families of lesser status served between 1645 and 1659, but they are untypical in many ways of the magistracy between the sixteenth and nineteenth centuries.
33. There was no shortage of Cheshire yeomen. Two sources which almost certainly underestimate their number list yeomen and gentlemen in a ratio of 3:2. These are the 754 men from whom Major General Charles Worsley exacted sureties of the peace in 1656 (Brit. Mus., Add. MS. 34013, fos. 2-55), and the list of active parliamentarians presented by a rigged jury in royalist Chester in February 1644 (Birmingham Reference Library, MS. 595611, 121-31). Without making a systematic search, I have been able to identify 700 yeomen families in lists compiled for other purposes.
34. Professor Everitt has suggested to me that marriage into an established gentry family might have conferred gentility. This is a possibility, but a survey of the rather sketchy genealogical evidence for the lesser gentry suggests that it occurred fairly infrequently.
35. Indeed, the grand juries' carousings were often disturbed. In 1628, as the jury sat down to supper, they found themselves confronted by an irate gentleman-litigant, himself flushed with wine, who proceeded to abuse them in word and gesture (C.R.O., Quarter Sessions Book 6a, f. 211). In October 1641, the jury was entertained by a troupe of minstrels whose offensive political ballads upset their digestion (P.R.O., Chester 24/126 no. 2, unfoliated).
36. There were 266 head constables altogether: 174 also served as jurymen, 128 before and 46 after they had served as head constable. A further 31

were included in jury panels but never sworn. Only 61 were never summoned for jury service, although some of these may have served before 1625 or after 1660. Sixteen of these 266 served in the office twice. For further details about the appointment and work of the head constables, in particular their heightened importance after 1646, see Morrill, op.cit., 237-9, and below, Appendix III.

37. It is also worth noting that trial juries were not drawn from the same panels as the grand juries but rather from quite separate panels.
38. For the history of the grand jury system, see W. S. Holdsworth, A History of English Law, vol. IV (1945 edn), passim, and A. Harding, A Social History of English Law (1966), passim.
39. Anon., The office of the Clerk of Assize (1682), 29-31
40. Cockburn, op.cit., passim.
41. Charges to the Grand Jury at Quarter Sessions 1660-1677, ed. E.M. Halcrow (Chetham Society, 3rd ser., vol. 5, 1953).
42. Grosvenor's charges are in a box of seventeenth-century Grosvenor papers now deposited in Chester City Record Office. I am grateful to Elizabeth Berry for drawing my attention to these documents, and to His Grace the Duke of Westminster for allowing me to use and quote from them.
43. P.R.O., Chester 24/131 no. 3, unfoliated. See also below, p. 43. The term 'presentment' was used at the time to describe the returns of defaults made by minor officials to monthly meetings or sessions. The use of this term was inaccurate and will offend the scruples of those educated in Angevin legal vocabulary, but it was the term in use at the time and I have been unable to devise a helpful alternative.
44. P.R.O., Chester 24/129 no. 3, unfoliated.
45. P.R.O., Chester 21/4, f. 292.
46. P.R.O., Chester 24/131 no. 1, unfoliated.
47. C.R.O., Quarter Sessions Book 7a, f.190.
48. P.R.O., Chester 24/125 no. 4, unfoliated.
49. P.R.O., Chester 24/128 no. 1, unfoliated.
50. See Appendix I.
51. For county policy towards bridges, see Morrill, op.cit., 241-3.
52. See below, pp. 31-2.
53. C.R.O., Quarter Sessions Book 7a, f. 112.
54. C.R.O., Quarter Sessions Book 8a, f. 54.
55. C.R.O., Quarter Sessions Book 10a, unfoliated.
56. P.R.O., Chester 24/129 no. 3, unfoliated.
57. C.R.O., Quarter Sessions Book 8a, f. 47.
58. E.g., P.R.O., Chester 24/131 no. 1, unfoliated.
59. No recusants were presented at quarter sessions between 1625 and 1640; partial returns (mainly for Wirral hundred) occur in five assize files during these years.
60. C.R.O., Quarter Sessions Book 8a, f. 109.
61. P.R.O., Chester 24/130 no. 4, unfoliated.
62. P.R.O., Chester 24/129 no. 2, unfoliated.
63. See above, p. 14.
64. C.R.O., Quarter Sessions Book 10a, unfoliated; P.R.O. Chester 24/131 no. 1, unfoliated.
65. C.R.O., Quarter Sessions Book 10a, unfoliated. The jury frequently drew attention to the qualifications of various local officials, another minor task which no other body was competent to do: See, e.g., P.R.O., Chester 24/122 no. 4, unfoliated, October 1634.
66. P.R.O., Chester 24/130 no. 2, unfoliated.
67. Chester City Record Office, unlisted Grosvenor MSS.
68. C.R.O., Quarter Sessions Book, 10a, unfoliated.

69. See Morrill, op.cit., 243-5.
70. P.R.O., Chester 24/130 no. 4, unfoliated.
71. P.R.O., Chester 24/131 no. 5, unfoliated.
72. C.R.O., Quarter Sessions Book 10a, unfoliated.
73. P.R.O., Chester 24/131 no. 2, unfoliated.
74. From the copy in C.R.O., Q.J.F.84 no 3, f. 180. But grand juries in other counties had taken action over weights and measures much earlier, during the Commonwealth. See for example, Henry Townshend's "Notes on the Office of Justice of the Peace", 1661-3, ed. R. D. Hunt (Worcestershire Historical Society, new ser., vol. 5, 1967), 117-18; Essex Record Office, Quarter Sessions Rolls, e.g. Q/SR 347, item 27; Q/SR 348, item 34 (Epiphany and Easter 1651).
75. P.R.O., Chester 24/129 no. 3, unfoliated.
76. P.R.O., Chester 24/132 no. 1, unfoliated.
77. P.R.O., Chester 24/129 no. 3, unfoliated.
78. P.R.O., Chester 24/127 no. 1, unfoliated.
79. P.R.O., Chester 24/127 no. 1, unfoliated. Those named were John Tilston for Broxton hundred (and for inclusion in the quorum); Peter Dutton for Broxton; William Massie for Nantwich hundred and the quorum; James Lowthian for Nantwich; Robert Gregg for Edisbury; Henry Birkenhead for Wirral and the quorum.
80. P.R.O., Chester 24/129 no. 3, unfoliated.
81. Chester City Record Office, CR 63/2/696, Arderne MSS., p. 61.
82. Clause 11 says, in part, that at every assize the grand jury was to 'present the names of persons to be made Justices of the Peace from time to time, as the county hath need... and at the summer Assizes to present the names of three persons, out of whom the kinge may prick one to be sheriff.' This clause also called for the grand jury itself to be 'chosen by and for the several parts or divisions of each county and not to remain at the discretion of the under-sheriff'. The Heads of the Proposals are printed in S. R. Gardiner, Constitutional Documents of the Puritan Revolution (3rd edn, 1906), 310.
83. Morrill, op.cit., passim.
84. P.R.O., Chester 24/127 no. 1, unfoliated; for the opposition to the raising of troops in 1648, see the letter book of Henry Bradshaw, Bodleian Library, MS. Top. e. 3, fos. 2-4.
85. P.R.O., Chester 24/131 no. 4, unfoliated.
86. P. J. Pinckney, 'The Cheshire Election of 1656', Bulletin of the John Rylands Library, XLIX, (1967), and Morrill, op.cit., 287-94.
87. Chester City Record Office, CR 63/2/702, Brereton MSS., pp. 39-42, numbered from the end.
88. D. S. Underdown, Somerset in the Civil Wars and Interregnum (1973), 149-51.
89. E.g., Cockburn, op.cit., passim; E. Andriette, Devon and Exeter in the Civil War, (1972), 57-9; D. H. Pennington and I. A. Roots, The Committee at Stafford, 1643-5 (1957), lxxxi, 342-4; The Diary of Henry Townshend of Elmley Lovett, 1640-1663, ed. J. W. Willis-Bund (Worcestershire Historical Society, 1920), vol. II, 110-224, passim.
90. C.R.O., Q.J.F. 70 no. 2, f. 10.
91. Brit. Mus., Add. MS. 36913, f. 60; Add. MS. 36914, fos. 220-1; Brit. Mus., Harl. MS. 2083, fos. 25, 46. For details of the political background to all the petitions, see Morrill, op.cit., chapter 2.
92. Or does not appear to have done. Brit. Mus., Harl. MS. 2173, contains a mass of documents relating to the Ship Money disputes, and although it contains petitions to the Privy Council from the justices, there is nothing from the grand jury.
93. C.R.O., Q.J.F. 74 no. 2, f. 19.

94. Chester City Record Office, Earwaker MSS., Box 35, The Humble peticon of the high sheriffe, justices of peace, grand and second inquest... . This collection is currently being resorted and reclassified.
95. P.R.O., Chester 24/132 no. 2, unfoliated.
96. The Humble Representation and Petition of the Justices and Grand Jury ... for the County Palatine of Chester, 16th May 1651. There does not appear to be a copy of this pamphlet in the Thomason Collection. The only copy known to me is in Chester City Library.
97. P.R.O., Chester 21/4, f. 327.
98. P.R.O., Chester 24/127 no. 2, unfoliated.
99. P.R.O., Chester 24/129 no. 2, unfoliated.
100. P.R.O., Chester 24/127 no. 2, unfoliated.
101. For a discussion of the changed role of the justices during the Interregnum, and the reasons for the change, see Morrill, op.cit., chapter 6.
102. See above, p. 12.
103. See above, p. 17. This list is by no means exhaustive and cannot be taken to mean that only a small minority of the minor Cheshire gentry were royalist.
104. There is an alternative explanation, but an implausible one. It could be argued that their inclusion was intended as a deliberate snub to men of such rank. This can be discounted partly in view of the above arguments, and partly because those named were only rarely fined for non-attendance. Had inclusion been understood as a calculated insult, they would surely have boycotted the sessions and submitted themselves to what was, for them, the inconsiderable fine of 40 shillings.
105. Oxfordshire Justices in the Seventeenth Century, ed. M. S. Gretton (Oxfordshire Record Society, vol. xvi, 1934), lxxxvi; Sussex Quarter Sessions Order Book, 1642-9, ed. B. C. Redwood (Sussex Record Society, vol. 54, 1954), xxiii.
106. B. W. Quintrell, 'The Government of the County of Essex, 1603-42' (Ph.D. thesis, University of London, 1965), chapter 2; Burne, op.cit., I, xxvii.
107. Cockburn, op. cit., 111-13.
108. S. and B. Webb, English Local Government: The Parish and the County (1906), 457.
109. Quintrell, loc.cit.; Surrey Quarter Sessions Records, 1659-1666, ed. D. L. Powell (Surrey Record Society, vol. XXXV, 1931), xii; Minutes of Proceedings in Quarter Sessions, 1563, 1574-92, ed. H. C. Johnson (Wiltshire Archaeological Society, Record Branch, vol. IV, 1948), xxi-xxii; Webb and Webb, op.cit. 455 ff.
110. B. J. Richmond, 'The Work of the Justices of the Peace in Hampshire, 1603-42' (M.Phil. thesis, University of Southampton, 1969), chapter 2.
111. Burne, op.cit., IV, xxiv.
112. Lincolnshire Quarter Sessions Minutes, 1674-95, ed. S. A. Peyton, (Lincolnshire Record Society, vol. 25, 1931), lxxi-lxxii.
113. Burne, op. cit. IV, xxii-xxiv; Redwood, op.cit, xi.
114. Quintrell, loc.cit.
115. Worcestershire Quarter Sessions Rolls 1591-1643, ed. J. W. Willis-Bund, pt II (1900), liv.
116. Burne, op.cit., II, xxxiii-v.
117. Anon, The Office of the Clerk of Assize (3rd edn, 1682), 102 (first published 1662, but probably written c. 1610); Warwickshire County Records, ed. S. C. Ratcliff and H. C. Johnson, vol. VI (1961), xxii; Burne, op.cit., II, xxxii; but see ibid., IV, xxiii, where Burne describes the jurymen as 'all freeholders below the grade of armiger and over that of smallholder'. The latter term is anachronistic though the meaning is clear.

118. Gretton, op.cit., lxxxvi; Lancashire Quarter Sessions Records 1590-1606, ed. J. Tait (Chetham Society, 2nd ser., vol. 77, 1917), 15; Willis-Bund, op.cit., liv; Richmond, loc.cit.
119. Quintrell, loc. cit.; Peyton, op.cit., lxx-lxxii; Redwood, op.cit., 10-11.
120. E.g. Cockburn, op.cit., chapter 6, passim; Willis-Bund, op.cit., li ff.; Powell, op.cit., I, xvii.
121. Quarter Sessions Records of the County of Northampton, ed. J. Wake, (Northamptonshire Record Society, vol. 1, 1924), passim; Willis-Bund, op.cit., li ff.
122. Ibid., xcix-c (my italics).
123. Webb and Webb, op.cit., 449.
124. Ibid., 449-53.
125. Gretton, op.cit., lxxxvii; Richmond, loc.cit.; Quintrell, loc.cit.;
126. The Diary of Henry Townshend of Elmley Lovett, ed. J. W. Willis-Bund (Worcestershire Historical Society, 2 vols, 1916, 1920), passim; Henry Townshend's "Notes on the Office of the Justice of the Peace, 1661-3", ed. R. D. Hunt, (Worcestershire Historical Society, new ser., vol. v, 1967), 68-137.
127. Hunt, op.cit., 84-5.
128. Ibid., 102.
129. Ibid., 117-18.
130. Ibid., 107.
131. Ibid., 97, 99-100.
132. Ibid., 83.
133. Willis-Bund, Diary of Henry Townshend, vol. II, 95-6 et passim.
134. Ibid., 110 ff.
135. Cockburn, op.cit., 113.
136. Sir James Astry, A General Charge to All Grand Juries (1725), 6.
137. See Morrill, op.cit., especially chapters 6 and 8.
138. For the distinction, see ibid., chapter 6. A principal source is the diary of Thomas Mainwaring, a Cheshire squire and active J.P. I am preparing an article on the importance of this diary, and hope to edit it.

APPENDIX I. A NOTE ON THE SOURCES

Cheshire is one of the few counties with really full records for both quarter sessions and assizes (or great sessions) from the mid-sixteenth century onwards. For the period under study, there exist all the order books for both courts, except for quarter sessions 1650-60; there are also almost complete sets of sessions files (or rolls) and much miscellaneous material. As a result 222 jury panels from the years 1625-59 have survived and there is a considerable number of bills of indictment in every file; quarter sessions indictment and presentment books exist for the whole period.

Assizes were held twice a year, and after 1629 two juries were sworn at every session. No great sessions were held during the years 1643-7 and the records for four sessions have been lost or damaged (autumn 1625 and 1659, spring 1649 and 1654). This leaves us with 103 panels for the years 1625-59. The quarter sessions files for 1625-42 are complete. There was then a gap of 30 months before the sessions held at Nantwich in July 1645. Between then and the end of 1647, continuing political instability led to several sessions being cancelled (one in 1646, two in 1647). From then until 1659 most sessions were held (except for one in 1653). One file for 1646 is missing, and two files lack jury panels (Easter 1655 and Easter 1657). Altogether 119 quarter sessions juries can be identified.

Most assize files contain both the full sheriff's panel, annotated to include last minute additions and absentees, and also the clerk's list of the jurors in the order in which they were sworn. The quarter session files usually contain only the sheriff's panel, marked to show who had been sworn and with little other information added. All give the christian name and surname, township or hamlet of residence and style of those impanelled: the number of emendations suggests that clerks and sheriffs were punctilious in their work.

The bills of indictment usually contain the true or ignoramus finding of the jury, but do not always do so. In the case of quarter sessions, there is a rough but incomplete overlap between the billa vera in the files and the contents of the clerks' indictment books.

Few quarter session presentments are to be found in the files. For the most part we have to rely on fair copies in the clerks' books. But assize presentments are to be found in almost all the assize files, complete with the grand jury's emendations. In about one-quarter of the files there are the chance remains of some of the raw material of presentments: the returns of petty or head constables, of churchwardens, commissioners of sewers, or even justices of the peace (in cases dealing with recusants or alehouses).

It has proved impossible to tabulate the contents of these presentments. An initial attempt to select suitable categories produced 32, many of which overlapped. Even if all the items could have been firmly placed, there would have remained many which ought to have been fully included in two or more different categories. There are also graver problems. Is a list of 88 recusants, presented by the grand jury on the basis of separate items from both head constables and two justices of Wirral hundred, to be counted as one, four, or 88 presentments? Similarly, should a list of 13 unmade roads taken from eight sources but gathered together under three heads count as three, eight, or 13 items? Faced with such difficulties, and with the probable need to produce a whole series of different calculations to support what could be proved by a narrative account, the attempt to quantify was abandoned.

There seems to have been no requirement for grand jury petitions to be preserved in the files. Only half of all petitions traced found their way into the court records. The others lie scattered amongst the public records and various family collections.

The order books for the two courts (particularly that of John Bradshaw for the 1650s) contain a number of regulations regarding grand juries. In this connection, it is particularly sad that the quarter sessions order book for the Interregnum years should be missing. Grand jury charges survive only in private collections, but at least we possess two excellent sets for the early and later seventeenth century. All in all, the Cheshire records in regard to grand juries in this period are hardly likely to be bettered for any other county.

APPENDIX II. STATISTICS

A. General

609 men sworn to at least one jury, 1625-59
199 men sworn to quarter session juries only
140 men sworn to assize grand and second inquests only
270 men sworn to juries at both assizes and quarter sessions
410 men sworn at assizes
469 men sworn at quarter sessions

164 men impanelled but not sworn at quarter sessions
308 men (estimated) impanelled but not sworn at assizes[1]
999 men (estimated) impanelled 1625-59[2]

497 families sworn to juries, 1625-59[3]
825 families impanelled, 1625-59 (estimate)

B. Hundredal distribution

The 609 jurors came from the following hundreds:

68 from Broxton hundred (henceforth BX)
117 from Bucklow hundred (henceforth BU)
91 from Edisbury hundred (henceforth ED)
59 from Macclesfield hundred (henceforth MA)
94 from Nantwich hundred (henceforth NA)
78 from Northwich hundred (henceforth NO)
66 from Wirral hundred (henceforth WI)
36 uncertain

The following demonstrates the pattern of selection at each of the sessions town and at assizes 1625-59):

	BX	BU	ED	MA	NA	NO	WI
Chester Q.S.	40	4	47	4	3	5	39
Knutsford Q.S.	2	90	6	17	13	15	0
Middlewich Q.S.	2	23	18	7	7	49	1
Nantwich Q.S.	12	19	14	7	70	21	3
Northwich Q.S.	3	28	23	2	6	34	3
Grand inquest	40	51	57	29	33	40	41
Second inquest	38	59	53	34	45	30	39

1. Based on samples from 1630-2 and 1650-2.
2. This assumes that 50 per cent of those impanelled but not sworn at quarter sessions were also impanelled at assizes.
3. See p. 48 n. 10.

C. Number of appearances at quarter sessions and assizes

609 men altogether:

165 men sworn once
96 men sworn twice
58 men sworn 3 times
52 men sworn 4 times
32 men sworn 5 times
35 men sworn 6 times
23 men sworn 7 times
17 men sworn 8 times
15 men sworn 9 times
10 men sworn 10 times
55 men sworn 11-15 times
24 men sworn 16-20 times
28 men sworn 21 times or more (see Appendix II E, below)

D. Recruitment to the juries

The following table shows the number of men serving for the first time on a jury at quarter sessions or assizes each year between 1633 and 1656. For the purposes of compiling this table, only the panels from 1618 onwards have been used.

Year	New jurors	Year	New jurors
1633	12	1645-7	25
1634	20	1648	33
1635	20	1649	20
1636	14	1650	23
1637	18	1651	12
1638	17	1652	20
1639	9	1653	22
1640	14	1654	19
1641	20	1655	18
1642	20	1656	24

E. Thirty leading jurors

The following lists those most frequently called upon to perform grand jury service, 1625-59:

Column 1 gives the hundred of residence (see Appendix II, B).
Column 2 gives the first and last year (during this period) in which the subject was sworn onto a jury.
Column 3 gives the total number of appearances on grand juries, 1625-59.
Column 4 gives the number of appearances at quarter sessions.
Column 5 gives the number of appearances at assizes.
Column 6 shows whether the juror served before 1625 (represented by 'a') or after 1659 (represented by 'b').

	1	2	3	4	5	6
Philip Antrobus	NO	1625-57	49	40	9	a
William Tomlinson	BX	1625-58	48	29	19	b
John Middlehurst	BU	1626-56	40	28	12	ab
Humphrey Page	MA	1625-42	40	29	11	a
Richard Whittingham	ED	1628-46	37	28	9	
John Francis	WI	1631-59	35	13	22	b
Philip Downes	BU	1625-48	32	24	8	a
John Edwards	BX	1626-43	32	6	26	a
John Kelsal	ED	1626-57	32	5	27	b
William Ravenscroft	NO	1625-59	31	28	3	a
Thomas Burroughs	NO	1625-59	29	18	11	ab
Alexander Duncalfe	BU	1625-41	29	12	17	a
John Horton	BX	1630-59	28	9	19	ab
Paul Wynington	NO	1625-42	28	5	23	a
George Bostock	BX	1626-42	27	0	27	
Thomas Littlemore	ED	1632-52	26	10	16	
Edmund Mouldsworth	BU	1626-48	26	18	8	a
Richard Edge	ED	1632-42	25	9	16	a
Peter Frodsham	BU	1629-53	24	13	11	
Thomas Gleave	BU	1625-40	24	11	13	a
John Smith	NA	1642-59	24	13	11	b
Randle Grafton	NA	1625-59	23	22	1	a
Edward Harper	BU	1625-38	23	8	15	a
John Hopley	BX	1631-51	23	8	15	
George Bradford	NO	1625-41	22	20	2	a
John Cotgreave	BX	1637-58	22	6	16	b
Richard Jeynson	ED	1639-58	22	7	15	
Randle Blackshaw	BU	1625-57	21	14	7	a
Richard Nangreave	ED	1640-59	20	4	16	
Robert Whittingham	ED	1626-41	20	7	13	

APPENDIX III. A NOTE ON THE HEAD CONSTABLES

This appendix is almost entirely based on the quarter sessions files and order books in Cheshire Record Office and on the Great Sessions Files in the Public Record Office.

Two head constables served in each of the seven hundreds of Cheshire; each hundred was subdivided, and each head constable took responsibility for a particular group of parishes and townships. Service as head constable might last for only 12 months or for a good deal longer. In the years before 1642, appointments were made by justices of each hundred at their monthly meetings, and each hundred followed its own traditions. For example, the Nantwich justices changed their head constables annually at their July meeting; the Wirral justices theirs in September. On the other hand, in Macclesfield, one successful head constable, Richard Wyche, served in one division for 12 years (1629-40) while four men served successively in the other division. Although appointments were made at hundredal level, appeals against appointment could be made to the full Bench at quarter sessions. Occasionally the justices ordered a constable to stand down, as in 1614 when they were told that Henry Hough was a man who held a 'freehould of landes exceeding small, and but in revercon, so small as suytes not to beare that office, and the more unnecessarie for him in regard his best meanes is by trading in comodyties being a shopkeeper'.

After 1646 the system changed; all head constables were henceforth appointed annually at Michaelmas quarter sessions. A further and more surprising development was that outgoing head constables themselves began to draw up short-lists of men they thought would make suitable constables; the Bench then made a final choice from these lists. All appointments were for one year only.

The most important duties of the head constables were fiscal. They co-ordinated the assessment and collection of local rates and some taxes. When the justices (for rates) or commissioners (for taxes) had allocated the total sum between the hundreds, it was the task of the head constables, in consultation with the petty constables of each township (not the parish in Cheshire) to divide the sum between the towns according to ancient ratings known as the 'Mize'. They were then responsible for driving on the petty constables to collect and return the sums thus assessed. The most usual and onerous of their duties concerned two local rates.

The first was a consolidated annual rate which was handed over to two county treasurers for poor prisoners in Chester Castle, for the upkeep of the house of correction (to which sturdy beggars, unmarried mothers, and other social nuisances were committed), and for maimed soldiers and war widows (of whom there were many as a result of the heavy Cheshire commitment to the Irish campaigns of the 1590s). In the late 1640s and 1650s this commitment was greatly increased by the parliamentarian casualties of the civil wars. The second rate was that for bridge repairs. Before the Civil War each hundred was responsible for the maintenance of its own bridges, so that collections in any particular hundred would fluctuate widely from year to year. But as a result of a ruling by John Bradshaw, in 1647 all bridges become a responsibility of the county as a whole, and the sums for bridge repairs in any given year were consolidated into a single rate. At the same time the head constables, who had hitherto simply enforced fiscal orders handed down to them at monthly meetings or sessions, were given some independent powers to view bridges, receive estimates from the stonemasons, and later, in some cases, to supervise the course of the repair or reconstruction. Although the head constables could not authorise a county rate, the Bench normally accepted their reports and estimates of the probable cost.

This is in fact only one aspect of the increased status of the post-war head constable. Whereas before the Civil War they were treated with scant respect and less consideration by the Bench, and were regularly threatened with imprisonment or heavy fines for failing to collect the whole rate on time, after 1646 they gradually became much more the partners of the justices, co-operating with them and seeking their support in battles with subordinates. The newly established power to nominate their own successors is a striking example of this. Whereas pre-war justices treated them exactly like petty constables, and made some former head constables serve in that lowly office, after 1648 all head constables were exempt from parochial or village work since they 'lived in a ranke far above the calling of a petty constable' [C.R.O., Quarter Sessions Book 9a, f. 107].

In 1651 they even became paid officials. This resulted from the development of permanent central government taxation. The Tudors and early Stuarts had received subsidies from time to time from Parliament, but by the early seventeenth century only a small percentage of the wealthier families were required to pay. The vast majority were free from exactions whose purpose was not essentially local. Charles I's regular recourse to Ship Money was more notable in that it had to be paid by a much larger section of the community than it was for its doubtful constitutional legality; it was certainly for the former that it was most hated in the localities. In Cheshire Ship Money was assessed in precisely the same way as the local rates discussed above. The head constables, indeed, had to bear the brunt of levying it and many of them were attacked with pitchforks by incensed yeomen as they tried to collect arrears. But worse was to follow. By the end of the civil wars Parliament had devised a new tax, the monthly assessment, payable by all householders, and the head constables were made responsible for supervising the work of the petty constables in collecting this regular tax, although problems of assessment were dealt with by special commissioners. In 1651 the head constables were granted a percentage of all they gathered in, so that they came to parallel the sub-commissioners of the other new sources of revenue, the Excise and Sequestrations. But their office was no sinecure; few head constables escaped being stoned, chased by dogs or otherwise abused by irate taxpayers.

Other general duties of the head constables were less important and rather spasmodic. For example, whenever the justices wanted to implement those sections of the poor law relating to watch and ward, the head constables were entrusted with the task of co-ordinating the operation in their own areas. Similarly in the late 1640s, when the severe shortage of grain led the justices to issue orders restricting the movement of grain and its conversion into malt, the head constables were asked to monitor the operation of the temporary restrictions.

Apart from all these duties, the head constables had overall responsibility for ensuring that the petty constables in their divisions performed all their duties, and they were supposed to be the principal watchdogs of village government. They were essentially the middlemen of local government, the drudges of the county executive. Had they done their work as an inspectorate better, they would have eradicated the need for extensive grand jury intervention in local government. But they appear to have commonly neglected their work in presenting defaults both to monthly meetings and sessions. Instead they themselves became the focus of a great deal of attention and criticism by the grand jury.